HOW TO READ MINDS & INFLUENCE PEOPLE:

The Science of Nonverbal Communication & Everyday Persuasion

Second Edition

CARL CHRISTMAN

Printed in the United States of America

Edited by Linda Stephens

Cover design by Lisa Knight

Guide Media, LLC
848 N. Rainbow Boulevard
#1421
Las Vegas, NV 89107

ISBN-13: 978-1511543880
ISBN-10: 1511543884

Table of Contents

HOW TO READ MINDS & INFLUENCE PEOPLE

Introduction

We are all sales people. Regardless of what your business card says, there is a very good chance that you have to work on a daily basis to sell people on something. To quote a line from Arthur Miller's play, *Death of a Salesman* (1949), "The only thing you got in this world is what you can sell. And the funny thing is that you're a salesman, and you don't know that." This selling may not have to be for a traditional product or service. Anytime you try to get people to accept an idea or do what you want, you are engaging in the age-old practice of selling.

Some of you are traditional sales people. Your daily goal is to convince as many people as possible to buy your company's product or use its service. You either get commissions or promotions based on how many sales you get and how much money you bring in. This accounts for one out of every nine workers in America or over fifteen million people. In fact, there are more people working in traditional sales positions than in manufacturing (U.S. Bureau, 2012). If you are among this legion of traditional sales people, then this book is definitely for you.

If you work freelance or are self-employed, this book is for you as well. Assuming you know what you are doing, odds are that providing the service to your clients is not nearly as challenging as getting the clients in the first place. You need to sell yourself to the clients and convince them they should hire you. This is often the most discouraging part of working for oneself. You probably did not plan on working in sales. You wanted to be a photographer, or website designer, or interpretive dancer. What you quickly discovered, however, is that the only way to pay your bills is to sell your service. If you are the best at what you do but cannot convince people to pay you to do it, it is still a hobby and you are still an amateur.

If you work in customer service or any job where you regularly come in contact with the public, then you, too, are working in sales. Modern companies are transitioning away from dedicated sales forces and expecting everyone to participate in the sales process. Every time you interact with customers, clients, or just members of the public, you are selling them on the fact that you know what you are doing, your organization is good, and their investment of time or money is worthwhile.

If you work for a business or organization but are not dealing with the public, this book is for you as well. The only way to work your way up the ranks and achieve your goals is to sell people on you. They need to believe that you are the best person for the position you hold and the best person for the promotion you want. With the uncertainty of the job market, keeping a job takes work. You cannot expect your boss or human resources department to clamor over you. It is up to you to take control of your career. This book will give you insights into how to do that.

If you do not have a regular job and want one, you are definitely in sales. Your job is to sell yourself to prospective employers. Résumés are your sales pitches, job interviews are the ultimate sales meetings, and you are the product. Your goal is to make the sale and get the best job possible with the highest pay and the best benefits.

If you are single and don't want to be, you too are in sales. Match.com profiles are your sales pitch and first dates are your sales meetings. You put your best foot forward and try to convince the other person that you are nice. As crass as it might sound, you are selling the other person on you. If you get a second date, the first one was apparently successful. If you wanted one, but didn't get it, then it is time to go back to the drawing board and deconstruct your sales technique.

If your work revolves around the selfless goal of helping others, sales is still an important component. As anyone in the medical field will tell you, diagnosing the patient is only half the battle. Getting him or her to follow medical advice and make the right health choices can often be a challenge. In other words, medical professionals are selling their patients on health. And therapists need to sell their patients on the best course of therapy.

Parents and teachers need to sell children on the best choices for their futures. Telling them to just do it is not nearly as effective as understanding them, getting inside their minds, and convincing them to take action. This book offers insights on exactly how to do that.

Lawyers sell juries on verdicts. Dentists get patients to floss. Clergy sell parishioners on salvation. Employees sell their bosses on raises. Bosses sell their employees on working harder. Lobbyists sell legislation to politicians. Politicians sell themselves to the public.

As you may have noticed, this book is for virtually everyone. We are all sales people. We all have to persuade other people. And we would all benefit from learning how to do this more effectively. One survey of over 9,000 workers found that employees spend an average of forty percent of their time trying to influence others (Pink, 2012). This does not necessarily mean they were engaged in traditional sales, where they made money by directly selling goods or services. Often they simply had to persuade others during the course of their work. This is what I have done for most of my teaching career.

As I was discussing this project with a friend, he was a bit skeptical. I told him that I was writing a book on sales and influence. He was incredulous and told me that if I had not made millions of dollars in sales, no one would take me seriously. He was focusing on the traditional notion of what a salesperson is. What he didn't see was that I have been working in non-traditional sales for the past dozen years. As a college professor I spend every day selling my students on the importance of education. When I reduce the number of absences, increase student retention, and help more students graduate from college, I am engaging in sales. I do not get a commission for every student that succeeds or a promotion if the school makes more money, but I am using the same principles that successful sales men and women use every day.

What sets this book apart from others on sales is its dual focus. Part one is all about the audience. How can we understand them better? In order to successfully get people to do what you want, you have to read their minds. You have to get inside their heads and know what they are thinking. They might be too polite, embarrassed, or humble to say what they really think about your product or service. Our job as sales people is to be mind readers.

The second part of this book is about how to influence people. How can we use time-tested psychological principles to move people in the direction we want? I cover both the keys to influence and the methods of influence. I will start by looking at the various principles that will help us create desire and lead people where we want. Then we will cover the actual steps necessary for an effective sales message. The same step-by-step strategy can be used when selling cars or selling a healthy diet; whether selling insurance or selling the value of education. It is not just about persuading them to believe, but getting them to take action.

As a professor of communications, I have spent years studying how language, psychology, and non-verbal communication work. By learning how to read people, especially my students, I found that I could get inside their minds. Just by looking at their faces I often knew exactly what they were thinking. In many of my classes I made it a habit to incorporate a little mind reading. This was a great way of getting the students involved in the class and illustrating some of the concepts we were discussing. Even though I showed them exactly how I did it and taught many of them how to read people, after a while I got the reputation of being the "psychic professor." As time went on I performed more and more for my classes. I soon realized that I needed to take my mind games outside the classroom and introduce them to others.

Thus began my career as a psychological entertainer. I was soon booked to perform for other schools, corporations, and civic organizations. By using this skill for entertainment, I eventually became a mentalist. For years I performed mind reading shows across the country. During the week I would teach my classes and on the weekends and in the evenings I would appear at the Magic Castle, corporate sales meetings, and other events.

Taking psychology, the power of suggestion, and mind reading to the masses has been an amazing experience for me. My goal here is to help you read people better and use that knowledge to influence them. What sets this book apart from others is the focus on audiences and what they are really thinking. By the time you finish, you will be well on your way to reading minds and influencing people.

Read Minds

Read Your Audience

The more you know about your customers, the better the encounters will be. People are far more likely to do business with people they like. And they are more inclined to like people that understand them.

There are several ways of learning about people. You can always research them ahead of time. With the plethora of information we have access to on the Internet, it should be easy to research almost anyone. What does their LinkedIn profile say? What do they say or "like" on Facebook? What else do they have online? This can be very effective, but it can be problematic if you learn things you should not know. If you share the wrong information, it can be awkward.

The second way to learn about a person is to ask questions and actively listen. As simple as it sounds, listening is a great way to get to know people. There is no trick to it. Ask questions and be genuinely interested in the answers. People love talking about themselves and having a real conversation is often overlooked in this fast-paced digital age. Emails and texts are no substitute for direct contact in creating a real bond.

Research on relationships and sales shows us just how important conversation can be (Cialdini & Martin, 2012). In a recent study, participants were divided into two groups. One group was told to be as efficient as possible and to hammer out a deal with the other party as quickly as they could. The other group was told to take their time and chat before they began. They were prompted to share some personal information and try to find something in common.

The first group was able to close the sale 55% of the time. The second group closed the sale 90% of the time. As you can see, spending the time to get to know your customer is a wonderful investment.

There are several things you can do above and beyond talking with people. They are techniques that will give you a true insight into the people you are dealing with. They include knowing the person's demographics, such as age and culture, understanding his or her personality and reading their facial expressions and other nonverbal cues.

There is a chapter later in this book that offers a detailed explanation of personality profiles and how to best sell to various types of people. There is also one on age and life phases. By understanding what people are facing based on their age you may know how better to address their concerns and make the sale. Finally, there is a chapter that explains how to read people's emotions by decoding their micro-expressions. If you can tell what people are really thinking, you are reading their minds.

I am going to assume that most of your prospective customers are from the same culture as you. For those that are not I have included an extra section at the end of this book that gives an overview of the major cultural variables. It also lists the measurements of those variables for most major world cultures and how you may best sell to people from those regions.

The chapter that follows is on cold reading. This age old technique of reading people will allow you to do a profile and figure out amazing things in a few seconds.

Cold Reading

Cold reading is a set of techniques used by psychics, mediums, and mentalists to glean information about someone they just met. It also allows them to relate to people as though they know their life stories and understand their needs and wants.

When used by psychics or mediums, this technique is typically shrouded in secrecy. They covertly employ it to make it appear that they have some sort of psychic insight into someone's past or are making a connection with a long-lost relative. They reveal things they "could not know" as a sign that they have real powers.

When mentalists use cold reading, we are generally more open about it. We reveal personal information about people in the audience without ever claiming that anything paranormal is going on. Some mentalists specifically tell their audiences that they are using cold reading. Others leave it vague, assuring people that they are using their keen powers of perception, which they are.

These cold reading techniques can also be used by the sales professional or anyone trying to persuade others. By knowing more about your customer or client, you have the edge. If you can read their mind and know their hopes, desires, and fears, you will have a much better chance of building rapport and ultimately making the sale. Here are some things to look for.

Clothing

Our clothing is an advertisement of how we want to be perceived. Whether or not we think about it, the way we dress tells the world a lot about us. Clothing can provide insights into style, values, and profession.

Obviously, a person who works in an office will dress differently than someone working in construction or in the hospitality field. When you look at their clothes, ask yourself what kind of work they probably do. Job-specific uniforms make this easy, but be careful not to use simplistic stereotypes. We might assume that someone who dresses formally is the boss. But the boss does not need to impress nearly as much as the employees do. Mark Zuckerberg is a good example of this. While the receptionist may have to dress up, the billionaire CEO can wear a hoodie or whatever else he wants.

Take note of the style. Is the person you are talking to trendy or not? Does it look like a lot of care went into getting the latest style or was this just what was available and clean?

Are the clothes ripped or stained, or do they look brand new? This often has more to do with values than with wealth. Someone who is less concerned with appearance and the approval of others will not dress as stylishly.

Pay attention to brands. Companies spend fortunes building their brands and making sure everyone knows the values they represent. If someone chooses to wear one brand or another, it is a pretty good indication of how he or she wants to be viewed. If a man wears Nike, he wants people to think he is athletic. If a woman wears Prada, she wants people to think she is wealthy. Whether or not this is true is an entirely different matter, but we can tell how people want to be perceived.

Something else to take note of is how the clothes fit and how flashy they are. If they are a bit tight, it might mean that the person recently gained weight. Conversely, if they are loose, they might have lost some weight. If the clothes are not the right size, it probably means that he or she is not overly concerned with physical appearance. If the clothes are flashy or overly revealing, it probably means that the person likes attention and is proud of his or her body.

Physicality

Pay attention to the physicality of the person you are speaking with. If they are especially fit, you can assume that exercise and diet are important. Is there a limp or other noticeable disability? This might be a clue as to what struggles someone is facing. What else do you notice?

Tattoos

Tattoos are fairly obvious artistic expressions. They generally represent people's experiences, passions, or loved ones. For most professionals, no tattoos will be visible, but when they are, it tells you a lot about what that person values.

Skin & Teeth

What do you notice about their skin and teeth? Do their teeth look like they had braces? This indicates that their family was at least middle class while they were growing up. Do they look like they have not been attentive to their teeth or could not afford dental care? How does their skin look? Are they pale from health issues? Do you see signs of a hard life or signs that they took good care of their skin? Have they spent a lot of time in the sun? Do you notice any scars and what do you think might have caused them?

Hair & Facial Hair

Also take note of what people's hair says about them. For men, a crew cut or buzz cut often indicates an affiliation with the military or law enforcement. Long hair is associated with being more artistic or individualistic. For women, is the hairstyle modest or bold? Does she want to stand out or not? If a man has facial hair, what is the style and how is it groomed? Is he trying to look professional, artistic, rugged, or something else?

Glasses

Glasses are no longer embarrassing. Today they have become a major part of fashion. By looking at the style of people's glasses, you may be able to tell if they are trying to look trendy, sophisticated, academic, or athletic? If you wore the same glasses they wear, how would you expect people to think of you?

Watch

Watches tell us a lot about people. The first question is whether or not they wear a watch. Now that virtually everyone has a smartphone and other electronic devices that tell time, many people no longer wear watches. If people wear a watch, it may mean that they don't like to rely on technology too much. It could also mean that time is very important to them and they check the time often.

The type of watch people wear is also significant. Expensive watches, like a Rolex, obviously signify wealth. Specific types of watches signify jobs or interests. Watches with multiple time zones indicate that someone is interested in travel. Dive watches, aviation watches, and those with stopwatches, tell a lot about what a person does. Digital watches show that a person is more practical and less concerned with fashion.

Lapel Pin

If men wear a lapel pin, there is a meaning. If he wears a flag pin, it is a safe bet that he wants people to know how patriotic he is. If he has a Rotary, Kiwanis or Lions club pin, he wants people to know how civically engaged he is. And if he has a school or company pin, he wants people to know how proud he is of that affiliation.

Jewelry

Jewelry and other accessories tell us a lot about people as well. There is generally a lot of symbolism behind them. Sometimes it is easy to identify. A medical bracelet is self-explanatory as is a crucifix or a Star of David on a necklace. The trick is to notice and identify what is right in front of you. The flashier the jewelry, the more attention the person wearing it wants. Expensive jewelry denotes wealth. The style of costume jewelry that someone chooses can show a desire to appear wealthy, creative, or even playful.

Rings

Rings are perhaps the most symbolic form of jewelry. People have been wearing rings for the past six thousand years to reflect status, show relationships, and reveal group affiliation. Not much has changed today. People still choose to wear one ring or another as a way of sharing their identity with the rest of the world.

Ring meanings are usually fairly obvious. An engagement ring and wedding ring are self-explanatory. A promise ring shows that someone is in a committed relationship, is generally younger, and is hopeful for the future.

Purity rings are part of a new trend. Some teens and young adults are starting to wear these as a sign that they will remain virgins until they are married. This generally shows that they want others to view them as virtuous and spiritual.

People who graduated from some high schools, colleges, or military academies may wear class rings. This shows that they are proud of the accomplishment and of that part of their lives. Signet rings that show a family coat of arms or membership in a fraternal order also give insight into what people value or how they self-identify.

Seeing that someone has a ring with a birthstone is also helpful. This naturally tells you when that person was born. Once you know their birthday, it can be easier to build rapport. If there is one stone, it generally represents that person's birth month. If there are multiple stones, they usually tell you the birth months of her children or even grandchildren. This is helpful in that it tells you how many children she has.

January – Garnet
February – Amethyst
March – Aquamarine and Bloodstone

April – Diamond
May – Emerald
June – Pearl, Moonstone, and Alexandrite
July – Ruby
August – Peridot
September – Sapphire
October – Opal and Tourmaline
November – Topaz and Citrine
December – Turquoise, Zircon, and Tanzanite

In addition to the birthstones by month, there are also birthstones based on astrological signs. If the person you are talking to is into astrology, he or she might use these. Although it is not as common as birthstones, roughly 30% of Americans believe in astrology (Harris, 2013).

Aquarius (21 January - 21 February) **Garnet**
Pisces (22 February - 21 March) **Amethyst**
Aries (22 March - 20 April) **Bloodstone**
Taurus (21 April - 21 May) **Sapphire**
Gemini (22 May - 21 June) **Agate**
Cancer (21 June - 22 July) **Emerald**
Leo (23 July - 22 August) **Onyx**
Virgo (23 August - 22 September) **Carnelian**
Libra (23 September - 23 October) **Peridot**
Scorpio (24 October - 21 November) **Beryl**
Sagittarius (22 November - 21 December) **Topaz**
Capricorn (22 December - 21 January) **Ruby**

Hands

In addition to rings, take a look at the rest of the hands. Do they look like the hands of someone that has done a lot of manual labor or someone who works in an office? Also, for women, do they have nail polish and, if so, what color? Nail choices (length, shape, color, ornamentation) can tell you how the person wants to be perceived: stylish, conservative, trendy, or flamboyant. There are also professions in which the use of nail polish is generally prohibited, for example nursing and food service.

Cold reading is an art rather than a science. No one of these signs can be taken as absolute proof of what kind of person you are talking with or what he or she values. Instead, view these as clues that give you possible insights.

Do not just assume that something is true. Use these insights as conversation starters and guides as you lead the conversation. Sometimes you might be wrong. But often you will be right. You will find that with practice, you will truly be able to get inside your customer's mind. After a while you will impress yourself with how much you know about them. (Rowland, 2008)

Stages of Life

One way to better understand people is to know where they are in the path of life. We generally like to think we are unique and different, and in some ways we are. In other ways, however, we are all very similar. Most people go through the same phases of life in the same general order. And most of us go through the same common life events at roughly the same ages. These life events include, leaving our parent's home, marriage, birth of a child, loss of a loved one, finding a job, promotions, retirement, and so on.

By knowing where someone is in life, what he or she is dealing with, and, more importantly, what is needed, you will have a much easier time building rapport. If you share the same gender, age and basic demographics, it will be fairly easy to relate. If not, it might be helpful to take a look at the general categories.

Gail Sheehy analyzed these stages in her seminal book *Passages: Predictable Crises of Adult Life* (1976). She found that people followed a predictable pattern as they aged, in spite of their differences. She described this pattern as stages that can roughly be divided into the decades of life, each with its own struggles and rewards. By understanding these common experiences, it is easier to address the common needs and challenges people have.

While issues like personality, which we will look at in the next chapter, may take a little time to figure out, age group is very easy to identify. It is possible to know a whole world of information about your potential customer before either one of you has spoken a word.

The Tryout 20s

The "Tryout 20s" ranges from eighteen to about thirty. This phase of life is generally characterized by two competing goals. The first is a desire for exploration and the second is a desire for stability. People in this age group are experiencing their first taste of freedom and often want to explore the outside world. They want to see what is going on outside the sheltered environment they grew up in. They still have the adventurous spirit of a teenager, but now may have the money and independence to actually explore.

As people leave their parents' homes and are forced to fend for themselves, they often feel exposed and desire a sense of stability. During this time they typically focus on getting an education and/or starting a career. Since they are starting at the bottom at work or are working temporary jobs until they finish their educations, there is not much stability.

Because they often have to move for school or work, they may live in temporary housing and not have a chance to put down roots. This is also the time when most people have their first serious romantic relationships and have children. During this decade, almost everyone deals with major life changes.

There have been some recent changes in this group. Although a third of people are living with their significant other, they are marrying later than in past generations. Men are marrying at an average age of 29, while women are marrying at an average age of 27. This is up from 26 for men and 23 for women in 1990. In addition, the average age for a woman to give birth to her first child is 25.5 and almost half of children are born outside of wedlock. (Hymowitz, 2013)

Part of this is because marriage is now being seen more as a capstone rather than a cornerstone. People want to be finished with their educations and have their careers established before getting married. In the past it was more likely to find a spouse to help in the process of establishing a stable life.

Tips for influencing people in their 20s:

Never talk down to this group. Emphasize their independence and power as consumers.

Be open to their consulting with their parents or others before making a purchase, especially a large one.

Focus on how your product or service will bring stability to their lives or will help ease the tension caused by some of their major life changes.

Emphasize how others in their peer group will approve of the purchase.

The Turbulent 30s

By the time someone reaches "The Turbulent 30s" he or she is firmly an adult. While those in their 20s may still turn to their parents for advice and support, by their 30s most people are more independent. By this age they often have their own children and identify more as a parent than a child.

By their 30s people are generally more established. They probably have a job where they feel more comfortable. They have been working for a few years and feel like they know what they are doing. They also have rent or a mortgage, car payments, and bills associated with their children.

They are starting to put down roots and feel pressure to stay where they are. Though they may want to travel the world and see new lands, that often feels out of reach. They find that with all of the commitments they have, they have less control over their time than they want.

By their mid-thirties people are conscious of getting older. Thanks to increasing life expectancy, the mid-life crisis that used to happen in the late thirties or early forties has now moved to the mid to late forties, but in the mid-thirties people are starting to become more aware of their own mortality. They are probably still healthy, but are starting to notice differences in their bodies. Although they do not feel old, they are starting to notice the toll of time. They are starting to see the end and beginning to question their purpose in life.

Because of this, people often feel the need for change. They may feel that they are stuck in a rut and question whether they want to stay on the same life course. This may include questioning their marriage or other relationships, questioning their career choices, or questioning how they spend their dwindling free time. They often feel trapped, unable to make changes, and yearn for something different. They longingly look back on the freedom they once had.

Tips for influencing people in their 30s:

Emphasize how your product or service will positively impact their family and children.

Make sure they see the purchase as being responsible, and not a mere luxury.

Focus on how your product or service helps them recapture the freedom or sense of adventure they once had.

Emphasize how the purchase signifies stability. It is not a short-term purchase (like a futon) they would have made in their twenties, but is a solid investment that will last (like a nice dining room set).

CARL CHRISTMAN

The Flourishing 40s

Even though people are living longer and middle age has been pushed to the mid to late forties, forty is still a major turning point for most people. There is a universal feeling that time is running out and that they need to hurry. People often feel that they are not ready to be middle aged and question where the time went.

There is an increased pressure to get things done. Those who are focused on their careers often push things into high gear as they try to get to the top before time runs out. Those who are not happy with their careers often choose this time to change jobs or go back to school. People may have the same existential questions they did in their 30s, but now they have more motivation and resources to take action.

Sheehy calls this period "middlescence" and says that it is "adolescence the second time around" (Sheehy, 1995). It is not unusual for people to feel the same kind of anxiety and tension they did in their early twenties. Instead of feeling uncertain about how to make it as an adult, however, they are now uncertain about what to do now that they have made it. They are uncertain about what to do with the rest of their lives.

The forties offer some unique challenges and some wonderful rewards. People in their forties are likely to earn more money than they ever have. This gives them the freedom to travel more, engage in hobbies, and make larger purchases. Their children are also old enough that they require less attention. This gives them far more time and freedom.

How people respond to this midlife change impacts the rest of their lives. Now that the children are grown or approaching adulthood, it is common to reevaluate marriages. Do they stick with their partner or look elsewhere? What do they do with the extra time not spent raising children? Do they focus more on their career or look for a change? How they answer these questions and how long they take searching for the answers often defines the forties.

Tips for influencing people in their 40s:

Emphasize how your product or service can help them make changes for the better or live up to their full potential.

People are likely to start buying things (furniture, electronics, and appliances) for the second time around, replacing worn out items. Emphasize how things have improved and what is new.

Explain how this purchase will bring them more esteem in their community.

You may justify your prices by establishing that they have worked very hard and that they deserve to do something for themselves.

The Flaming 50s

The fifties are often marked by acceptance, confidence, and renewal. By the time people reach their fifties they are firmly planted in the new phase of life. Unlike the forties, where there is often a sense of loss as one moves from young adulthood into maturity, by the fifties, people usually embrace the new phase. There is less worry about what others think and the authentic self can emerge.

The health issues that come with old age have not yet set in, but the years of experience are evident. Sheehy calls this period "The Age of Mastery." With the midlife crisis starting to ebb, people are often confident in what they have learned and accomplished. There is an increased emphasis on their role as a mentor or leader. Many in their fifties relish sharing their knowledge and experience with others.

During this time people start looking toward transitioning out of the workforce. Some look forward to it, while others dread it. Those, especially men, who define themselves based on their profession, will often be forced to redefine who they are. As people look toward retirement, one of the most common questions is, "what do I really want to do with my life?" New passions often emerge. Travel, artistic endeavors, volunteerism or other hobbies start to receive more attention.

For many, this is the time to face existential questions. They have time to ponder the meaning of life and reevaluate who they are. Some turn to their religion for these answers, while others become more spiritual. There are questions about the purpose of one's life up to this point, but also, how one makes a difference in the future.

As the role of a parent ends, for many the role of caregiver for their aging parents begins. They are forced to start renegotiating their role with their parents. This preview of their future also raises questions about their future health, how they will deal with their children, and whether they will have enough money to survive through retirement.

Tips for influencing people in their 50s:

Be open to input and suggestions from them as they share their experience.

Make sure they understand the long-term value of your product or service.

Emphasize the minimal long-term commitment. People do not generally want to be stuck making payments into retirement.

Emphasize how your product or service will have a positive impact on the community, including children and grandchildren. How does it allow them to spend more time on the important things or with the important people in their life?

The Serene 60s and Beyond

The sixties are not what they used to be. When Social Security was established in the 1930s, the life expectancy was 58 for men and 62 for women (Calculators: Life Expectancy). Now it is 84 for men and 86 for women. People are living a lot longer with a better quality of life (Life Expectancy). Those in their sixties today can generally expect to have many years of productivity ahead of them.

This once homogenous group now has a variety of paths to choose from. Some people continue to work as long as possible, out of either necessity or a love of their work. Some continue working part-time to stay busy. This gives them a smoother transition to retirement and allows the company to retain some of their expertise. Some turn to volunteerism or a new career. And some choose the standard path of retirement.

This phase of life presents new challenges. For those who worked hard for the past few decades, it can be difficult to adjust to a more leisurely life. Also, being with one's partner all the time can be a new and frequently challenging experience, since work and other responsibilities probably occupied much of their time in the past.

Assuming people have saved enough, this phase of life can offer more freedom than they have ever had. Travel, time with grandchildren, and hobbies can be very rewarding. Research shows that people in their early twenties and late sixties are the happiest. By the time people reach their sixties, they are usually more comfortable in their skin, and free of many of the pressures they dealt with throughout middle age.

In the seventies and beyond, more attention is generally focused on health. Staying healthy, spending time with family, and engaging with community become very important. Existential questions about the meaning of life take center stage and people often look longingly toward past experiences.

Tips for influencing people in their 60s and beyond:

Focus on tradition and make sure they know that your brand or organization has been around for a long time.

Emphasize the durability over the flashiness of your product or service.

Highlight the customer service they will get and the long-term nature of their purchase.

Take your time and do not rush things.

Personality Traits

Our minds are complex. If I wanted to really get to know you, I would have to spend hours talking with you. I would get to know what you like and dislike, how you interact with others, and how you view the world. Aside from friends and family, we seldom have the time to get to know people this well.

It is helpful to have a shortcut that helps us understand people more quickly. That is exactly what personality profiles are for. Personality tests are attempts to make sense of the complex human psyche. If we can quantify and categorize it, this makes it easier and more efficient to understand people. Instead of having to spend hours or days talking with them, we can understand them in a fraction of the time.

There are countless personality profiles out there. They are basically different people's ideas about how to quantify the complex human mind. They range from the pop-culture quizzes like "What Sex and the City Character are You?," (I am a Samantha); "What Color Best Describes You?," (I am plaid); or "What Animal are You?," (I am a duck-billed platypus) to more scientific ones. Perhaps the most commonly known personality profile is the MBTI® or Myers-Briggs Type Indicator (Keirsey, 1998).

The Myers-Briggs' personality profile helps us find order in seemingly random human behaviors. When we understand a person's personality, their actions are no longer random. We discover that there is a reason for most things they do. More importantly, we can better understand how to persuade them. We are going to start with an explanation of the four spectrums, eight options, and sixteen personality types. We will then look at how to apply these personality differences to the sales process.

Instead of trying to memorize the sixteen personality differences, which could prove difficult, it is easier to start with the conceptual framework. By understanding how personality measurement works, things should fall into place. Myers Briggs is based on four separate spectrums. People are not just one or the other. They fall somewhere along the continuum. They are:

Extraverted --- **Introverted**

Sensing --- **iNtuition**

Thinking --- **Feeling**

Judging -- **Perceiving**

Since people usually fall toward one side or the other of each of these spectrums, this gives us a total of sixteen personality types.

ISTJ	ISFFJ	INFJ	INTJ
ISTP	ISFP	INFP	INTP
ESTP	ESFP	ENFP	ENTP
ESTJ	ESFJ	ENFJ	ENTJ

There is no need to know each one of these personalities. We are going to focus on the four spectrums. If we understand how those work, the specific personality traits should make sense. Once we understand these basics, we can see how they relate to sales and influence.

Extraverted vs. Introverted

We can have two distinct types of focus. We focus on the outside world of experiences, activities, and other people. We also focus on the inner world of thoughts, ideas, and imagination. Both of these focuses exist to some degree in all of us, but most of us have a preference for one or the other. Our dominant trait is either to focus on the inner world, and be *introverted*, or to focus on the outer world, and be *extraverted*.

Extraverted	**Introverted**
Acts first and reflects or thinks about it later	Thinks about it first before taking action
Needs to be around others and feels deprived when cutoff or when alone for too long	Needs to have alone time and feels overwhelmed when around groups for too long
Motivated by the outside world and what other people think	Motivated by internal desires and goals regardless of others
Likes to be a social butterfly and talk with many people	Likes one-on-one interactions and prefers smaller groups

Sensing vs. Intuition

There are two distinct ways of categorizing and organizing information. We make sense of the world around us by focusing on our five senses and what things look and sound like today. We also make sense of the world around us by looking for patterns and the possibilities of tomorrow. Both ways of understanding exist in all of us, but most of us have a preference for one or the other. If we are more concrete, we call it *sensing*. If we are more abstract, we call it *intuition*.

Sensing	Intuition
Focuses in the here and now and on current opportunities	Focuses on future possibilities and opportunities
Tends to be more practical and use common sense ideas to solve problems	Tends to be more imaginative and use creative ideas to solve problems
Remembers things in detail based on the five senses	Remembers contexts and patterns based on feelings
Improves best from past experience	Improves best from theoretical understanding
Prefers clear and concrete information	Is comfortable with ambiguous information

Thinking vs. Feeling

There are two distinct ways of processing information. We analyze things in a logical, detached, and objective way. We also analyze things in a more emotional, interpersonal, and compassionate way. Both of these types of analysis exist in all of us, but most of us have a preference for one or the other. If we are more analytical, we call it *thinking*. If we are more relationship oriented, we call it *feeling*.

Thinking	Feeling
Naturally focuses on logic and looks for facts when making a decision	Naturally focuses on feelings and how a decision will impact others
Focuses more on tasks that need to be finished	Focuses more on the needs and desires of other people
Much better at giving objective opinions and analysis	Much better at finding consensus and popular opinion
Accepts conflict as being a natural part of relationships	Is often bothered by conflict and tries to keep the peace

Judging vs. Perceiving

There are two distinct ways of organizing our lives and getting things done. Sometimes we like to plan things out in detail ahead of time. Other times we like to take life as it comes and act on the fly. Both of these ways of handling things exist in all of us, but most of us have a preference for one or the other. If we are geared more toward planning, we call it *judging*. If we are more geared toward multitasking, we call it *perceiving*.

Judging	Perceiving
Prefers to plan many of the details before taking action	Prefers to improvise and take action without a plan
Prefers to focus and finish one thing at a time	Prefers to multitask and have a variety of things going on
Works best without pressure and prefers to avoid deadlines	Works best under pressure and when there are deadlines
Prefers to schedule things and use commitments to organize life	Prefers to avoid commitment and keep things open and flexible

If you have one type of sales pitch, it is likely to work on one kind of people. But as you can see, there are many types of people with many different types of personalities. The more you are able to tailor your message, the better your odds of relating to your customer or whomever you want to influence.

Everyone has a way they would prefer to be dealt with. Unfortunately, they will not tell you what it is. If you recognize the clues, however, it will be much easier to build rapport, influence them, and ultimately get them to take action.

There are two problems. First of all, it is not usually possible to figure out all of these personalities during a brief interaction with a customer. It generally takes either a bit of time or an actual personality test to figure it out. It is not as simple as memorizing sixteen different influence techniques and then applying the right one to the right person. You will encounter a lot of ambiguity.

Because of this, I only apply one or two personality dimensions during each phase of the influence process. This makes everything much easier.

Understanding your own personality is as important as understanding that of others. If you would like to take an online personality test to find out more about yourself, go to: www.CarlChristman.com/Personality

Building Rapport

In the initial phase of any interaction, sales or otherwise, it is important to build rapport. To have a good relationship, you must create common ground and make sure that your customer actually likes you. The only personality trait we care about for the initial rapport-building phase is introversion vs. extraversion.

If you are working in traditional sales, odds are that you are extraverted. The people you are dealing with, however, may not be. Building rapport with extraverts is fairly easy. If you notice that they are talking more loudly and quickly and are enjoying chatting with you, they are probably extraverted. If this is the case, all you need to do is match their level of energy to build the relationship.

If they are more reserved, speak more quietly or slowly, or stand farther away, there is a good chance they are more introverted. Just because they are more reserved, it does not mean they do not like you or want to deal with you. To create rapport with an introvert, just slow down and give them time to think. Also give them space to feel comfortable. They are more likely to be comfortable if you match their energy level.

Needs & Information

Once you have built rapport, it is time to move on to actually selling your product or service. You need to understand the person's needs and explain how you can help satisfy them. It is up to you to persuade him or her and the best way to do that is to understand his or her personality. For this phase of the sales process we will be focusing on sensing vs. intuition and thinking vs. feeling. Since there are two dimensions and each has two options, this gives us four possible types of people. If you can tailor your pitch to each of these four types, you will have a greater chance of success.

Intuitive Thinkers:

This type of person wants unique and innovative solutions. They value products and services that are outside the box. They will often be concerned about the long-term implications of the deal and will want to know how your product or service holds up over time. They might even pose complicated "what if" type questions. This does not mean they are not interested. They just want to make sure they cover all the bases. Be confident and bold in your presentation. Make sure you take plenty of time to address their hypothetical questions and emphasize how unique your product or service is.

43

Intuitive Feelers:
This type of person wants a solution that fits with their pre-existing ideas and is personalized. They are less interested in innovation than comfort. They also want to feel like the presentation is individualized. If it sounds like you have delivered the same spiel a thousand times, you are likely to lose them. They are likely to go with their gut and want to make sure that everything feels right. They are likely to want to explore a variety of options, if only hypothetically. They might also talk about their hopes and dreams for the ideal product or service. Make sure you engage their imagination and embrace their vision. They are more likely to do business with someone that understands and embraces their ideas.

Sensing Thinkers:
This type of person just wants the facts laid out in a logical and straightforward fashion. They are likely to ask concrete questions about specific details. They will probably want to know about things like cost, delivery, warranty, and other policies. Expect them to get into the nitty-gritty of the deal. Make sure you are able to address their concerns. They are not going to be making a decision based on how it feels. They will act based on whether all of the details line up and the deal makes logical sense.

Sensing Feelers:
This type of person wants the facts, but they want them in a personalized manner. Even though the facts do not change, they want to know that they are presented to them in a personalized way. They are more likely to be loyal to a product, brand, or even salesperson. They will want to know how the product or service will benefit them or people they care about. Make sure you focus on their practical concerns and their needs. If they like you, they are more likely to stick with you.

Call to Action

The final step is obviously the call to action. In this phase all we care about is the judging vs. perceiving personality trait. Even once you have convinced your customers that your product or service is the best, you still have to get them to take action. The judging vs. perceiving trait is the single biggest predictor of how and how fast they do this.

Judgers are more likely to make quick decisions. They prefer to take action sooner rather than later. They like the idea of having things settled so they can move on to something else. If you have persuaded them that your product or service fulfills their needs, the deal should close itself. In some cases, the customer might even push things along and tell you they are ready to finish things up.

Perceivers do not like being tied down or locked in. They want plenty of time to explore their options and make sure there is not a better deal they are missing. Just because they are resistant to committing does not mean they are not sold on your product or service. They just hate the idea of committing to something, especially if it is long-term. Make sure you give them plenty of time and do not pressure them. If you apply too much pressure, they are likely to resist and you might blow the deal. They are moving in the same direction, just at a slower pace.

One way of improving your odds with perceivers is to offer money back guarantees, trial periods, or shorter-term contracts. They are no more likely to cancel or ask for their money back, than judgers, but they like the freedom. There is no need to offer these options to everyone, but it is a good idea to have them as backups when it becomes clear that you are dealing with a perceiver.

By understanding the way your customer prefers to be dealt with, you will both have a much better experience. There is no need to have a one-size-fits-all approach based on your own

45

personality. If you do this, you will probably do great with people who are similar to you and struggle with those who are not. There is no reason to change who you are, but with a few simple tweaks you can customize your approach for the person you are trying to persuade.

The more you play with personality profiles and the more you focus on listening to your customer or client, the easier this will become. At first you might have to actually think about what you are doing and consciously adjust your behavior to fit with their preferences. After a while, however, you will find that this all becomes second nature. Just matching their energy and decision making styles will be easy. (Brock, 1994)

Facial Expressions

The face is by far the most expressive nonverbal communication channel. It has the most complex system of signaling on the human body. Because of this, scientists spend more time studying facial expressions than non-verbal communications in other parts of the body. And the general public instinctively values face-to-face communications over written or electronic forms. (Matsumoto, Frank, & Hwang, 2013)

The emotions we express on our faces tell our stories to the world. No matter how hard we try, our real emotions are bound to come out at some point. What sets nonverbal facial expressions aside from verbal communication is that there are multiple continuous channels of communication that are often unconscious.

While speaking, people may choose when to start or stop a message and will only have one channel of verbal communication to control, meaning that they can only say one thing at a time. With nonverbal communication, however, the individual will always be communicating many different messages simultaneously, often without conscious thought.

It therefore takes much more effort to control nonverbal messages. Professional poker players have long understood the power of tells. Skilled players can often determine when their opponent is bluffing just by looking at what they do nonverbally. By understanding how to read people's faces, you will have a powerful advantage in any sales situation, since you will be able to glimpse thoughts and feelings that remain unspoken.

Emotions

Emotions are complex systems of feelings we all experience. Many people spend their entire lives trying to make sense of their emotions or the emotions of others. Many books have been written in an attempt to quantify the range of human emotions. Here we will quickly look at emotions and how they pertain to reading people in order to improve the odds of influencing them.

Emotions can be seen as physiological, since they influence the way our bodies act. Emotions can be seen as psychological, since they are rooted in our minds. And emotions can be seen as social, since they are intrinsically tied to those around us.

Emotions are very useful, since they help us rapidly process information and respond with little or no conscious thought (Tooby & Cosmides, 2008). Many human experiences are so common that we have evolved to have intrinsic emotional responses. When faced with rotten food or bodily fluids, we do not have to stop and ponder whether or not these might be dangerous. We instinctively feel the emotion of disgust. When a wild animal is racing toward us, we do not have to analyze the situation. We immediately feel the emotion of fear and are ready to fight or flee.

These emotions save us time, prevent our having to analyze every situation, and times save our lives. Our instincts show that our unconscious selves are a step ahead of our thinking minds. Emotions are created as we look around and instinctively analyze our environment. Emotions help us control our behaviors and make decisions.

Although the specific triggers for these emotions might be different in various cultures, the overall emotions are universal.

Studies have been done in which participants were shown pictures of people from other cultures and were asked to rate their emotions (Elfenbein & Ambady, 2002). They were able to read the emotions written on people's faces across cultures. In other research, congenitally blind people exhibited the same emotions and corresponding facial expressions as sighted people (Galati, Sini, Schmidt, & Tinti, 2003). Even though they had never seen another human face, they instinctively responded the same ways when feeling the same emotions.

There are countless human emotions, but researchers have identified seven basic universal types of emotions: anger, contempt, disgust, fear, sadness, surprise, and happiness. These emotions are found in every culture and people generally exhibit the same facial expressions when they feel them. They are biologically innate. Even babies express these universal emotions the same as the rest of us before they have had a chance to learn how they should respond.

Anger

Anger is usually triggered when someone or something stands in the way of achieving an important goal. It can also be caused when someone perceives an injustice or a violation of social norms. The non-verbal response generally includes the eyebrows being drawn together as the eyes glare. This is caused when the upper eyelids are raised as the lower eyelids become tense. The lips are also tightened. Anger prepares people to fight or do whatever is necessary to remove the obstacle that stands between them and their goals.

1. Eyebrows down and together
2. Eyes glare
3. Narrowing of the lips

To see a video example go to:

www.CarlChristman.com/Emotion/Anger

Contempt

Contempt is triggered when people perceive something or someone as being inferior. They feel superior and view the other as being of less value. The non-verbal response is generally a one-sided smile or tightening of a corner of the lips. While anger is a more active emotion that prepares people to fight, contempt is usually more passive and serves only to show that one feels a sense of superiority.

1. Lip corner tightened and raised on only one side of the face

To see a video example go to:

www.CarlChristman.com/Emotion/Contempt

Disgust

Disgust is triggered when people feel revulsion to something they perceive as unpleasant or offensive. The non-verbal response is to wrinkle the nose or raise the upper lip. Both of these actions create a scrunching of the middle part of the face. This is a common response when people are around spoiled food, bodily fluids, or anything else nasty. The purpose of disgust is to help people avoid contamination.

1. Nose wrinkling
2. Upper lip raised

To see a video example go to:

www.CarlChristman.com/Emotion/Disgust

Fear

Fear is triggered when people perceive a threat to their physical or psychological well-being. The non-verbal response includes widening of the eyes and stretching of the lips horizontally. The eyebrows are generally drawn together as the upper eyelids are raised and the lower eyelids are tensed. The purpose of this emotion is to prepare people for fight or flight, so it helps people stay safe.

1. Eyebrows raised and pulled together
2. Raised upper eyelids
3. Tensed lower eyelids
4. Lips slightly stretched horizontally

To see a video example go to:

www.CarlChristman.com/Emotion/Fear

CARL CHRISTMAN

Sadness

Sadness is triggered when people lose something or someone that is valuable to them. It can be los of concrete things like a house or a car, personal relationships like a friend or lover, or abstract things like self-esteem or confidence. The non-verbal response includes raising the inner corners of the eyebrows and dropping the upper eyelids. It also includes a lowering of the corners of the lips. Sadness allows the mind and body to slow down and conserve resources, while the loss is being dealt with. It can also serve as a call for help.

1. Drooping eyelids
2. Losing focus in eyes
3. Slight pulling down
   of lip corners

To see a video example go to:

www.CarlChristman.com/Emotion/Sadness

CARL CHRISTMAN

Surprise

Surprise is triggered by sudden and unexpected actions or objects. The non-verbal response is a raising of the eyebrows and the upper eyelids. The jaw is also usually dropped, leaving the mouth open. Surprise is generally the briefest of emotions. As the novelty of the situation wears off, so does the emotion. It often leads directly into other emotions, such as happiness (if it was a good surprise) or anger (if it was a bad surprise). The purpose of the surprise emotion is to help people process information.

1. Eyebrows raised
2. Eyes widened
3. Mouth open

Only lasts for about a second

To see a video example go to:

www.CarlChristman.com/Emotion/Surprise

Happiness

Happiness is triggered by achieving a goal. People generally feel happy when their needs are being met. The non-verbal response is raising the corners of the lips, raising the cheeks, and narrowing the eyes. The purpose of this emotion is to motivate people to achieve further goals and work toward things in their best interest.

1. Crow's feet wrinkles
2. Pushed up cheeks
3. Movement from muscle that orbits the eye

(Ekman & Friesen, 1978)

To see a video example go to:

www.CarlChristman.com/Emotion/Happiness

Macro-expressions are the large facial expressions that are easy to identify. They involve the entire face and usually last from 0.5 to 4 seconds (Ekman, 2003). When people show macro-expressions, they are generally not making any attempt to hide it. They are feeling one emotion and they are happy to let others know what it is. We can all easily identify these facial expressions.

Micro-expressions, however, are much more subtle. These involuntary expressions are generally very hard to control. They happen when someone is trying to hide their emotions or has conflicting emotions. Micro-expressions happen in a half second or faster and generally only involve a part of the face (Ekman, 2003).

For example, if you give someone food that you made, he or she might momentarily exhibit micro-expressions that show disgust. The desire to not hurt your feelings, however, might cause him or her to exhibit a larger macro-expression of joy so as not to hurt your feelings.

Or customers might view your proposal with contempt. If they express that, however, they know that you will spend more time explaining it and trying to persuade them. In an attempt to expedite things, they might try to hide that emotion. By knowing that you do not have the prospective customer on your side, you can quickly change your pitch and hopefully turn the interaction around.

How do you do this? The next chapter will focus on empathetic accuracy, intuition, and how to use what we have discussed to actually read people.

Empathetic Accuracy

Have you ever felt as though you knew exactly what someone else was thinking? If so, it may have felt like mind reading. What it was, however, was what psychologists call empathetic inference, the process of ascribing specific emotions or feelings to people based on their non-verbal cues. Empathetic accuracy is the extent to which this is successful (Ickes et al., 1990).

William Ickes, one of the leading researchers on this topic, has called this, "everyday mind reading" (2003). In this process we use nonverbal cues to help us understand what another person is thinking. This may seem like a supernatural occurrence, but it is something so innately human that even babies can do it.

This ability begins at birth. Research shows that newborns prefer looking at human faces as opposed to other stimuli. When they are only a few weeks old, babies are able to imitate facial expressions. At two months old, they are able to recognize and respond to the emotional states of their parents. By one year old, infants carefully watch the facial expressions of adults and use them to guide their interactions. As children grow, they become more and more perceptive.

Every part of life is improved by having this ability to read the emotions of others. Empathetic accuracy is positively correlated with improved peer relationships, work relationships, and even romantic relationships. When it comes to peer relationships, research has found that those with better empathetic accuracy have more and healthier relationships (Gleason, Jensen-Campbell, & Ickes, 2009). When it comes to work, those who are able to read others tend to have better relationships and, therefore, be more successful.

In romantic relationships, empathetic accuracy is a key indicator of relationship satisfaction. In stable relationships, people are generally able to read their partner's thoughts and understand their feelings. (Simpson, Ickes, & Blackstone, 1995). Those who can figure out their partner's needs are better able to meet those needs, whether those needs are social support or material things (Verhofstadt, et al., 2008).

These three factors that often diminish empathetic accuracy: being a psychopath, being autistic, or being a man. One of the key factors in defining someone as a psychopath is their inability to empathize with others (Decety & Skelly, 2013). Luckily, you are not likely to meet many true psychopaths. Autism is also characterized by an impairment of empathetic accuracy. It is harder for those on the autism spectrum to read the emotions of those around them (Roeyers, et al, 2001; Baron-Cohen, 2009). You are likely to know people with some level of autism. Finally, research shows a negative correlation between testosterone and empathetic accuracy. The higher the testosterone level, the less likely a person is to be able to read the emotions of others (Ronay & Carney, 2012). You almost certainly have to deal with men.

Women are marginally better at reading people, especially when the gender differences are highlighted. When researchers told subjects that they were focusing on gender differences, women did better. This implies that women focus more on the emotions of others when they are reminded of the gender stereotypes concerning women's intuition (Ickes, Gesn, & Graham, 2000). Men and women did about the same when financial motives were included. When people were told that they would receive rewards if they successfully read others, men did better than normal (Klein & Hodges, 2001). This shows us that men and women are both able to read others. It also shows that with effort people can improve their empathetic accuracy.

There are several things that help people to be good mind readers: familiarity with the subject, a desire to understand, a good sender, and feedback. We will touch on each of these aspects and actually practice reading people.

The first key is familiarity and comfort with the person you are trying to read. People have a much easier time reading people they know well (Colvin, et al, 1997). Knowing someone well gives you a baseline from which to start. You already know their personality and how they typically act. You are looking for what is different. Since you lack this context with strangers, reading them is a bit more challenging.

The other reason it's easier to read friends is that they are generally more open with their emotions. They are less likely to repress their feelings because of social protocol. When we are around strangers we try to put our best foot forward. When we are with friends, we can be ourselves.

The second key is to understand the other person and to have an actual relationship. In a piece of research that I am sure will not surprise you, men and women were found to be much better at reading members of the opposite sex when they perceived the other person as interesting and attractive (Ickes, et al, 1990). Obviously, the more people like others and want to get to know them, the more energy they will put into understanding what they think and how they feel.

People are more likely to focus on others when they want to establish or maintain a relationship (Pickett, et al, 2004). This is a very important point. If we are focused only on making the immediate sale, we are likely to be less perceptive and overlook the real feelings of our customer. If we are focusing on building a long-lasting relationship, however, it is easier for us to be in tune with what they are thinking. Obviously, a real relationship and true understanding should be the goal.

The third key has nothing to do with you. It is all about the other person and how easy they are to read. There is a spectrum of emotional expressions for individuals as well as cultures. Just think about how easy children are to read. They have not yet learned the social rules and how to hold back or hide their emotions. This is why you can look at most children and know exactly how they feel and what they are thinking.

Some people are naturally more emotionally expressive than others. Emotionally expressive people are less likely to suppress negative feelings (King & Emmons, 1990). When they are unhappy, disgusted, or afraid, they let others see it. Emotionally repressive people are more likely to try to hide their feelings. People often smile just to be polite and hide their negative feelings. (Ansfield, 2007; Hecht & LaFrance, 1998) This is where having a history with people can be helpful. If you are aware of their expressiveness, you will have a better idea whether they are just being polite or are really expressing how they feel.

In addition, people from some cultures are predisposed to show more positive emotions and repress negative ones, even in times of trouble (Ekman & Friesen, 1969). For many in these cultures, the desire to follow proper social etiquette trumps the open display of emotions. The extra section on culture at the end of this book sheds light on some of these important cultural differences.

The good news is that, with some effort and feedback, empathetic accuracy can be improved (Barone, et al, 2005; Marangoni, et al, 1995). The problem is that it is often hard to get feedback during normal interactions. It is a bit awkward to tell people what you think they are thinking and then ask them if you are right. This kind of procedure certainly doesn't fit well into most conversations. This is, however, exactly what I have done when trying to improve empathetic accuracy.

There are several ways of getting this feedback. The original method that researchers used was to record two people having a conversation. They would then take the participants into separate rooms and ask them to watch the video. As they did, they were asked to stop the video whenever they remembered having a specific emotion. The researcher logged the specific thought or feeling at that precise time.

Once this was done, the participants watched the video again. This time the researcher stopped the video at every point where their counterpart had noted thoughts or feelings. The participant was then asked what he or she thought the other was thinking or feeling. The researchers then compared the sender's response with the receiver's response. The closer they were, the better the empathetic accuracy. (Ickes, et al, 1990; Ickes & Tooke, 1988)

By giving people feedback after they have tried to read the other person, their empathetic accuracy typically gets better. Although the researchers' method is very effective, it takes a lot of work and infrastructure to do. The technique we are going to use involves taking pictures of individuals as they are thinking about specific things or feeling certain emotions. These feelings or thoughts are recorded along with the picture. The receiver, you, will look at the pictures and try to figure out what the person in the picture is thinking or feeling.

This will be a little more challenging than what the people in the original studies faced. They had the advantage of knowing the people they were trying to read and had a baseline of their emotional expressions. You will probably not know the people in the pictures. But this will be a bit easier, because there will be multiple-choice answers for you to choose from, at least in the beginning.

Now that you know about the major human emotions and corresponding facial expressions, forget about them. Do not try to analyze every micro-expression. Go with your gut and rely on your intuition. As Malcolm Gladwell (2005) pointed out in

Blink: The Power of Thinking Without Thinking, our snap judgments made by our unconscious mind are often more reliable than our well-reasoned and deliberate decisions. As he put it, "We need to respect the fact that it is possible to know without knowing why we know and accept that - sometimes - we're better off that way." We do not have the time or mental energy to analyze every interaction we have with others.

Our unconscious minds are amazing in their ability to quickly decipher the thoughts and feelings of others. You need to arm yourself with an understanding of human emotions, facial expressions, and nonverbal cues, which you have already done. Then you need to trust your instinct and make minor adjustments where necessary.

Rather than trying to learn anatomy and focus on each muscle in the face to decipher what it means, the most efficient method of reading minds is to simply mirror the other person. Ask yourself how you would feel if you looked the way that person does. Put yourself in their shoes and try to feel what they are feeling. We are going to try a quick experiment to see how this works. Take a moment to study the picture below and then go to the next page.

Now I have one simple question for you. On which side was the clock? This is not a trick question and it should be fairly easy to remember. The point of this question is to make you think about your perspective. You have a picture of me playing poker with a group of dogs (I love Photoshop). Because I am facing the camera and you are facing me, what side is the clock really on? Did you say that the clock was on your right or my left? Either answer is correct. The point is to get you thinking about the world from the other person's perspective. Put yourself in the other person's shoes and ask yourself what he or she is experiencing.

Starting on the next page, you will see pictures of people's eyes, the most expressive part of the face. Put yourself in their shoes and ask how you would feel. Which of the four choices best describes their emotion? Write down your answers. At the end, you will be able to score yourself.

This test is not timed, but try to go as fast as you can. Carefully analyzing the pictures will generally not help. Go with your instinct. If you cannot identify it right away, it is unlikely that more time will help.

As a sample, look at the image below and choose which emotion you think this man is feeling.

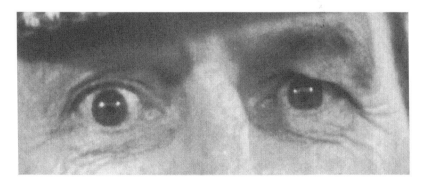

jealous – panicked – arrogant – hateful

If you chose "panicked," you are correct.

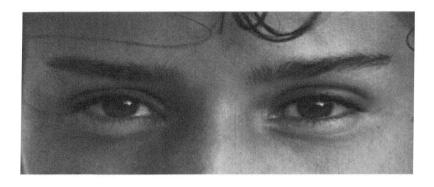

1.　playful – comforting – irritated – bored

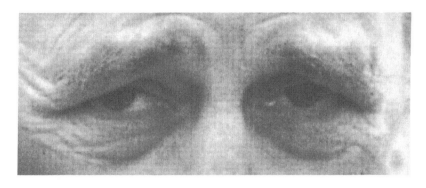

2.　terrified – upset – arrogant – annoyed

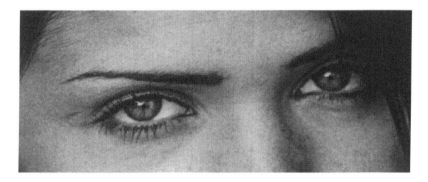

3.　joking – flustered – desire – convinced

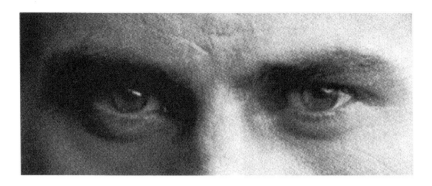

4.   joking – insisting – amused – relaxed

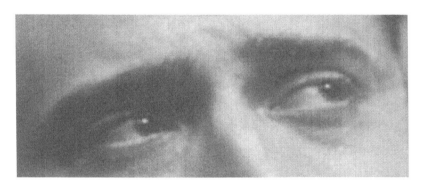

5.   irritated – sarcastic – worried – friendly

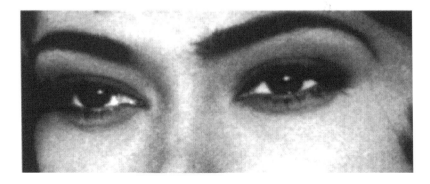

6.   aghast – fantasizing – impatient – alarmed

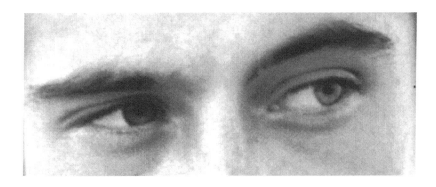

7.   apologetic – friendly – uneasy – dispirited

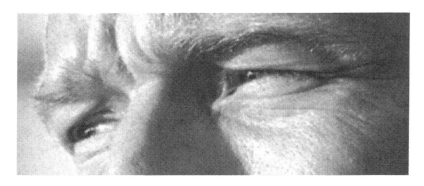

8.   despondent – relieved – shy – excited

9.   annoyed – hostile – horrified – preoccupied

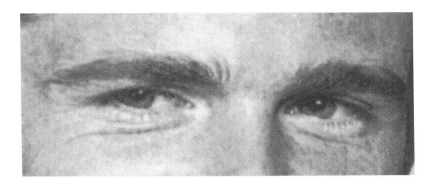

10.　cautious – insisting – bored – aghast

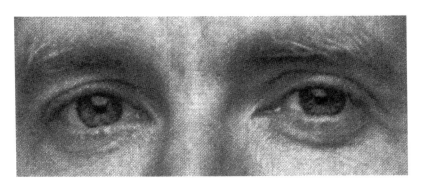

11.　terrified – amused – regretful – flirtatious

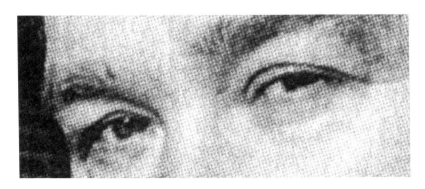

12.　indifferent – embarrassed – skeptical – dispirited

Compare your choices to the answers listed below and see how many you got correct.

1.	playful	7.	uneasy
2.	upset	8.	despondent
3.	desire	9.	preoccupied
4.	insisting	10.	cautious
5.	worried	11.	regretful
6.	fantasizing	12.	skeptical

0 – 6   You have difficulty accurately reading people.
7 – 10   You have an average ability to read people.
11 – 12 You are very good at reading people.

This test is courtesy of Simon Baron-Cohen and his colleagues at the University of Cambridge (Baron-Cohen, Wheelwright, & Hill, 2001).

As I mentioned before, reading people is a skill that can be improved with practice. In the extras section of this book you will find two additional tests like this one. To improve your ability to read people's minds, go over the ones you missed on this test and try out the new tests at the end. You may also take these tests online by going to:

www.CarlChristman.com/Empathy

Take a look at the iconic pictures that follow and see if you can figure out what these people were thinking or feeling.

CARL CHRISTMAN

What do you think Salvador Dali was
thinking or feeling in this picture?

What do you think Florence Thompson
was thinking or feeling in this picture?

What do you think Che Guevara was
thinking or feeling in this picture?

Influence People

Coercion vs. Persuasion vs. Compliance Gaining

Before we delve into influence, we need to define our terms. Persuasion is often used as a catchall term for anything relating to changing the minds or actions of others. But what exactly does "persuasion" mean? Does it matter why people change? Do actions matter more than beliefs? And don't you hate it when people start off with a list of rhetorical questions?

Coercion, persuasion, and compliance gaining are often used interchangeably. Persuasion is the act of getting someone to change his or her beliefs. Coercion is when this is accomplished with force or threats. And compliance gaining is when people actually take action. My goal in the second half of this book is to help you avoid coercion, become a master of persuasion and ultimately achieve compliance.

If we look at the stereotypical sleazy car salesperson, pushy telemarketer, or annoying door-to-door huckster, we can find numerous examples of coercion. If your only goal is to make the sale, coercion often works. If you pressure enough people, some of them will invariably bend to your will. For most, however, this is a big turn off and likely to end the relationship.

Coercion is most effective when you will only have a one-time interaction. Once the customer escapes, it is highly unlikely that they will return and subject themselves to such abuse a second time. My worst job, and one of my most memorable experiences, was as a car salesman. While I was in graduate school, I decided to spend a summer putting my academic study of influence and human nature to the test on a car lot. In those brief months, I learned more from real salespeople than I learned from many of my professors.

Aside from quite a few crude jokes, there were two things my sales manager taught me. One was that you can never trust the customer. The other was that if they left the lot, they were never coming back. One blisteringly hot summer day in Moreno Valley I was dealing with a customer, a nice guy that was interested in an SUV and just wanted to look at a couple of models. I gave him a full tour of the SUVs he was considering, recited my spiel about the bells and whistles, and took him on a test drive. When we finished, he said he liked it, but he would have to check with his wife. With that he proceeded to leave.

I headed back to the main building, content with the job I had done. My sales manager, however, was not impressed. He ran over to the man and intercepted him before he was able to leave the premises. He told the man that we would not be getting any more of that vehicle in stock before the next model year came in and the prices went up, which was false. He told him that there were other people coming to take a look at it that afternoon and this might be his last chance, which was false. And when the man insisted that he needed to get his wife's input before making such a large purchase, my manager insisted that she would be proud of him for getting such a good deal, which sounded very unlikely to me.

There was no physical force, but by twisting his arm and pushing him to do something he was not comfortable with, my manager was using a form of coercion. Perhaps this is why car salespeople are consistently ranked as some of the least honest and least ethical people around. According to a 2013 Gallup poll, only 9% of people ranked car salespeople as being trustworthy. The only professions that came in lower were members of congress and lobbyists. That is not an especially high bar to clear.

Honesty / Ethics in Professions (Gallup, 2013)

82% - Nurses	29% - Auto mechanics
70% - Pharmacists	27% - Bankers
70% - Grade school teachers	23% - Local officeholders
69% - Medical doctors	22% - Business executives
69% - Military officers	21% - Newspaper reporters
54% - Police officers	20% - Advertisers
47% - Clergy	20% - State officeholders
46% - Day care providers	9% - Car salespeople
45% - Judges	8% - Members of Congress
32% - Nursing home operators	6% - Lobbyists

I have no doubt that my sales manager was correct: After leaving our dealership, that customer was not likely to come back. Unfortunately, by making the sale in the way he did, the sales manager created another set of problems. First, the customer was likely to face a rightfully angry wife at home, since he spent a large amount of money without discussing it with her. Second, because the decision to buy resulted from a great deal of pressure, the customer is very likely to regret his decision. As a result, the customer is not only unlikely to return to that dealership, he is likely to tell everyone he can that they should avoid that business. The negative effect of that coerced sale ripples through time.

As we all know, it is easier to keep the clients or customers we have than to get new ones. If the customer associates his new vehicle, the dealership I worked for, my sales manager, and me, with a negative experience, he is unlikely to come back. In the short-term, coercion worked. On that day many years ago, thanks to my manager's tenuous relationship with the truth, I made a good commission. In the long run, however, coercion is not very effective. I can't imagine that he would have returned for his next purchase or recommended us to his friends.

Another reason that coercion is a poor tactic is that the balance of information has changed in the customer's favor. This approach to making a sale would only work on a low information buyer. When I worked in the car dealership, we were not allowed to take calculators into the sales rooms. The managers did not want the customers to be able to check on the misleading figures they were getting. If they offered an estimate of the payments per month, plus the down payment, plus the trade-in value, they did not want the customers to know how much they were actually paying in the end.

Of course, this was before the advent of smart phones and few people carried around calculators. Now everyone has one. In addition, people have a whole world of knowledge at their fingertips. If they want to know when the new models come out, they can look it up. If they want to know the invoice price, they can find out. And if they want to know what competitors are charging, they can just search. The days in which sellers can monopolize information is coming to an end and attempts to use coercive sales techniques are increasingly doomed to failure.

Persuasion, as opposed to coercion, works much better. There is no shortcut to honest persuasion. If people, without being excessively pressured, choose to listen to you, you have succeeded. If that man had consulted with his wife and they had both been honestly persuaded that they should buy, not only would we have made the sale, we also would have had a much better chance of winning customers for life. When she needed a new vehicle, we would have been their first stop. When their friends needed vehicles, they would have recommended us.

With the techniques we are going to cover in the next few chapters, persuasion is actually pretty straightforward. As you will see, changing minds is the easy part. What is difficult is changing actions and behaviors. Convincing people to believe something is simple. Getting them to take action is harder. So, while persuasion is the first step, compliance gaining is the ultimate goal. We don't want people to do things they don't want to or don't believe in. That would be coercion. But it often takes a little push to get people to go from merely believing to taking action. Our job is to motivate action.

There are countless examples of people who want to do something, but for some reason haven't done it yet There is no one in America who doesn't understand how unhealthy smoking is, yet there are tens-of-millions of Americans who still smoke. Persuading them that smoking is bad is not the issue. Getting them to act on their own desire to stop smoking is.

Far more people want to exercise than actually do. More people want to eat a healthy diet than do. Everyone knows that they should save enough for retirement, but most people don't. And many more people want to make positive life changes than ever follow through.

As any campaign manager will tell you, persuading voters that their candidate is the best choice is only part of the battle. The real challenge is getting them to actually go out and vote. Countless elections have been won or lost based on "get out the vote" campaigns. The ground game of making sure people remember what day to vote, know where their polling place is, and even offering to drive them there, is crucial.

Compliance gaining is key to all forms of influence. For traditional sales, convincing people that you have the best product is pointless if they don't take that final step and actually buy. And convincing them you have the best service is irrelevant if they don't follow through and use it.

Compliance is equally important for other professions. Healthcare workers' lives would be significantly easier if patients actually took their advice. A significant portion of medical research is devoted to determining how to increase patient compliance. In the United States alone up to 40% of patients do not adhere to their doctor's recommendations and 125,000 deaths a year are attributed to a lack of compliance (Atreja, Fellow, & Levy, 2005). If doctors could find a way of influencing more patients to follow the treatments they prescribe, countless lives would be saved.

Teachers' jobs would be much easier if their students would do what they are supposed to. If teachers could get more students to do their homework and show up for class, dropout rates would plummet. Persuasion is only the first step. Telling students what they need to do is easy. The trick is to get them motivated enough that they are willing to put in the hard work necessary to succeed. In my many years teaching, I found that I have two jobs. The first is to teach the class. The second is to help the students stay motivated and engaged, so that they are more likely to succeed.

Just giving an assignment and the necessary information seldom works. The more I make students want to learn, study, and succeed, the better the classes turn out. What I have to do is show them how my class will help them succeed in life and give them the gentle nudge they needed to further their education.

In my opinion, this is the key to influence. It is a combination of persuasion and compliance gaining. Make sure people know what they want and then help them get it. The next chapters will help you accomplish this.

Keys to Influence

The human psyche is complex; fortunately, it is also very predictable. By understanding the principles of persuasion and the keys to influence, we can greatly increase our chances of bringing about desired change in people. There is never a guarantee that any one of these techniques will work, but they can certainly increase your odds.

Think of them as tools. You will never use all of them, but they are handy to have in your persuasion tool bag. For some audiences and for some messages, one tool might work better while in other situations another might be the key. When using the right tool with the right message and the right audience, it can make a huge difference.

Legions of social scientists have spent years researching the psychology of influence and armies of sales people have spent years testing their conclusions in the field. Most notably, Dr. Robert Cialdini (1984) identified six keys to influence. I have condensed the keys to influence to four with the acronym S-A-L-E (Social proof – Authority – Likability – Exclusivity).

We will look at the science behind these psychological principles and examples of how they have been successfully used. But more importantly, we will look at how you can use them to achieve your goals and influence those around you.

Social Proof

"If everyone else jumped off a bridge, would you?" We have all heard this somewhat clichéd argument against giving in to peer pressure. The truth is that we do look for social proof when deciding what to do and what to believe. The principle of social proof is basically that we tend to determine what to think based on what others think and we tend to choose the best course of action based on the choices we see others make (Aronson, Wilson, & Akert, 2012).

Despite what your parents may have told you about the dangers of following your friends, there is some wisdom in taking our cues from others. Our brains have evolved to use social proof as a cognitive shortcut. Let's imagine that you are in a building and all of a sudden you see everyone else frantically running for the exits. Are you going to sit around and analyze the situation to figure out why they are running and determine the best course of action? Or are you going to put your brain on autopilot and run with them? In many cases, we have a better chance of survival when we heed social proof.

There are definitely problems inherent with our automatic reliance on social proof. Fear often spreads like a pandemic when people take their cues from their peers rather than the experts. Americans have been driven to hysteria over health threats such as anthrax, small pox, bird flu, swine flu, mad cow disease, and Ebola. In each of these cases public health officials struggled in vain to reassure the public, but their proclamations were no match for the social proof. If most of my friends are scared, there must be a good reason and therefore I should be afraid as well (Siegel, 2006).

Luckily many people have harnessed this human tendency to make the world a better place. Let's start by saving the environment. If hotels can get guests to reuse their towels during multi-night stays, they will have less laundry to wash. This is good for the environment as well as their bottom line. The question is how can we get more people to take this simple step of reusing their towels. A group of researchers (Goldstein, Cialdini, & Griskevicius, 2008) decided to tackle this issue by using social proof and ran a test to see if they could get more people to comply. They arranged to have a hotel put two types of signs in their rooms. In half the rooms they used a standard sign that emphasized the environmental impact of their actions.

> HELP SAVE THE ENVIRONMENT. You can show your respect for nature and help save the environment by reusing your towels during your stay.

In the other half of the rooms they used a sign that offered social proof that others were doing it and asked them to follow along.

> JOIN YOUR FELLOW GUESTS IN HELPING TO SAVE THE ENVIRONMENT. Almost 75% of guests who are asked to participate in our new resource savings program do help by using their towels more than once. You can join your fellow guests in this program to help save the environment by reusing your towels during your stay.

They found that an additional nine percent reused their towels when shown the second sign, rather than the first. The simple action of pointing out that others are doing it is enough to get many to take action. The same thing was discovered when looking at recycling rates. The researchers found more people chose to recycle when they were told how many of their neighbors did (Schultz, 1999).

Fundraising often works better when there is social proof. Telethon hosts keep telling people how many others have donated. Many organizations have done well putting together public events like "Walk for the Cure" or the "March of

Dimes." And in 2014 the "Ice Bucket Challenge" went viral as a way to raise money for amyotrophic lateral sclerosis or ALS. People were encouraged to film themselves pouring a bucket of ice water over their heads and post it in online, challenging their friends to do the same. Almost lost in the publicity stunt was that people were supposed to make a donation to the ALS Association as well. In spite of this oversight, they were able to raise over $115 million in a few short months (Silverman, 2014).

Social proof is of special importance when it comes to public health. Many of our health habits, both positive and negative, revolve around social interactions. There are many social smokers and social drinkers. People are more likely to start smoking as a result of being around others who smoke and binge drinking is most often done in social groups.

If you want to reduce binge drinking among college students, one of the easiest ways is to surround them with peers who do not drink. (Weitzman, Nelson, & Wechsler, 2003). And if you want people to quit smoking, get the people around them to quit. People are much more likely to give up smoking when their friends, family members, or spouses quit as well (Christakis & Fowler, 2008). Even though everyone knows that smoking and binge drinking are unhealthy, the social proof coming from those around them is often hard to overcome. Harnessing that social proof makes it easier to improve public health.

92

For most of us, eating is a social activity. We are likely to eat the same general kinds of foods as those around us. We will probably also eat as often as they do, at the same times, and similar portion sizes. This is why one of the best ways of improving overall health is with things like workplace wellness programs. Being told that we should eat healthy, lose weight, and exercise in order to avoid threats to our health is not nearly as powerful as being put into a situation where everyone around us is doing exactly that. The social proof that is fostered with these group health programs does wonders in influencing people.

Social proof can be equally helpful when it comes to education. I often use it in my classes to motivate students that are falling behind. I have found that sometimes pointing out the consequences can be helpful, but the students generally already know they risk failing. A far more effective method is to tell the student how everyone else is doing in the class. If they missed an assignment, I will point out that ninety percent of the class turned it in. If they do not do their reading and do not do well on the subsequent quiz, I will tell them how they did in comparison to the rest of the class. More often than not, this form of social proof motivates students and is a useful tool in promoting student success.

Let's move on to the part that everyone who works in traditional sales roles has been waiting for. How can social proof be used in making sales? We are going to see how everyone from infomercial writers to street performers use social proof. We will see how it can be used online and off and how it can be used to sell food or get dates.

Colleen Szot gives us one of the best examples of harnessing social proof for marketing. She is a leading infomercial writer who was able to drastically increase sales by changing one line. The standard call to action was something along the lines of, "Operators standing by, call now." She changed it to, "If operators are busy, please call again"

(Dworman, 2003). On the surface this line seems counterintuitive. It is telling people that they might have to put up with an inconvenience to place their order. The brilliance of this simple change was that it established social proof. If operators are standing by, that implies that they are just sitting around getting bored. Their being too busy to take our calls implies that a lot of other people are already calling, which indicates that it is a popular product. If it is popular, it must be good.

This is why it is good for bars, nightclubs, and restaurants to have lines. Nightclubs will often allow people in slowly so there is a line outside. If they let everyone in all at once, the establishment would not look popular from the outside. Many restaurants have found that it is in their best interest to adjust their prices to the point where there will be more demand than supply. Let's imagine there is a restaurant that has reservations booked for weeks in advance or there is a physical line in order to get in. Since the demand outpaces supply, they might be tempted to raise their prices. That, however, could diminish their very visible social proof. If they raised their prices, fewer people would try to get in. If fewer people tried to get in, that would imply that it was not as popular and therefore not as good. When faced with two restaurants, one with a line and one that can seat you right away, most people would rather wait a little bit. After all, if there is a line, it must be good food. All those people can't be wrong.

McDonalds proudly announces "Over 99 Billion Served" as their social proof. If they have served more burgers than there are people on Earth, it must be good. But McDonalds also spends over a billion dollars a year telling people how good they are through advertising (About McDonald's, 2013). Where I live, in Southern California, In-N-Out Burgers spend virtually nothing on advertising. Their 290 locations rely instead on social proof. What stands out most about their small drive-thru locations is that they almost always have very long lines of cars waiting to get through. Whereas McDonalds builds larger locations where they can serve many more people per hour, by keeping things small and having the lines outside, In-N-Out makes sure that everyone knows how popular they are.

Whether they realize it or not, everyone from street performers to those trying to find a date use social proof. All cultures rely on social proof, though collectivistic cultures are more impacted (see extra section on culture for more information) (Bond & Smith, 1996). Street performers and others who make a living from tips have discovered the power of salting the tip jar. If people see a full tip jar, they are more likely to believe that tipping is the standard thing to do. The hardest part is to get the first tip, so it's best to start by putting some money in your own tip jar, preferably bills. Which of these tip jars would you be more likely to contribute to?

Social proof can be a valuable tool for people looking for a date. If you show up at a bar with a group of friends, especially of the opposite sex, this shows other people that you are a nice person. It tells them that there are people who like you and implies that they should, too. In online dating, people who show pictures of themselves in groups are more attractive to prospective dates. Having a group of friends in the picture shows others that he or she is a good person and worth getting to know. This picture, if it were real, would show that I have friends and am a nice guy.

Successful Internet marketers have learned how to harness the power of social proof. Hotels.com has constant popups that tell you how many people in your area are using their website and when people reserve a room. This information is utterly useless in helping you find a room, but it's priceless when it comes to establishing social proof and showing customers that the website is popular.

99 people are currently looking at hotels in
Los Angeles

Product reviews on Amazon and views on YouTube are a form of currency. The more people that view your video or endorse your product, the better off you are. And Yelp reviews can make or break a company. Showing potential customers that other people are visiting your business and like it is one of the best ways to entice them to do the same.

If you want to get higher prices for things you sell on eBay or other auction sites, harness the power of social proof. Instead of starting with a higher price, closer to what the product is actually worth, start with a ridiculously low price. The lower the price, the more people will bid on it. The more people that bid, the more popular it looks. The more popular it looks, the better it looks. And the better it looks, the more money it's assumed to be worth. (Ubel, 2008)

While going through my library I found multiple copies of the same book and decided to put this to the test. I put one on eBay with a starting price of $10.00. The other one had a starting price of $1.00. The one I listed at $10.00 ended up having three bids and sold for $8.50. The one I listed for $1.00 ended up having seventeen bids and sold for $14.25. This is a small sample size and a minor change, but it shows the power of social proof.

People are more likely to take their cues from people who are similar to them (Abrams, et al., 1990). If you are trying to influence college students, telling them what people their parents' age would do will not be nearly as effective as telling them what their peers do. Sharing the same gender, race, culture, age, religion, politics, or citizenship are important. Even tenuous similarities that we would not normally identify as being important to our identity can have a huge impact.

After finding that people were more likely to reuse their hotel towels when social proof was used, the researchers decided to take the study a step further. In another experiment they tested to see whether pointing out similarities with others would increase the power of social proof. They tried out various messages that emphasized citizenship or gender, but the most effective one turned out to be one that emphasized the similarity of having stayed in the same room (Goldstein, Cialdini, & Griskevicius, 2008).

> JOIN YOUR FELLOW GUESTS IN HELPING TO SAVE THE ENVIRONMENT. In a study conducted in Fall 2003, 75% of the guests who stayed in this room (# insert room number here) participated in our new resource savings program by using their towels more than once. You can join your fellow guests in this program to help save the environment by reusing your towels during your stay.

Having simply stayed in the same room does not seem like it would have much of an impact on people. After all, they have never met these people and have no idea whether they have anything in common. Nevertheless, the more focused the group, the more effective they are as social proof.

If you want to get people to quit binge drinking, stop smoking, or live a healthier lifestyle, it is better to show them what people similar to them are doing. When I want my students to do better in class, I don't point to students in general but to their peers. Some similarities are built in. People searching for hotels in the same city, shopping for the same product on Amazon, or bidding on the same product on eBay have something in common.

Nothing, however, can compare to the power of friends. Facebook, Twitter, and other social media platforms have changed the sales landscape. It is now easier than ever to find out what our friends and family members like. If they like something, that social proof can have a real impact. If they are willing to offer an actual testimonial, all the better. This is why it is so important to ask for endorsements.

Help your customers out and make their social media recommendation as easy as possible. Do not expect them to gush about your product or service on their own. Give them content to like or comment on. If you can create a blog post, picture, or video that is compelling, they will share it. If you can spark a discussion that they care about, they will tell others. Social proof is a wonderful tool and social media puts it within reach of everyone willing to invest the time.

The most important person one looks to when trying to decide what to think or do is one's self. People tend to do what they have always done. And they tend to stick with what they already believe.

In the 2004 United States presidential race, John Kerry was famously labeled a flip flopper after he tried to explain his support for the Iraq and Afghanistan wars. He said, "I actually did vote for the $87 billion, before I voted against it" (Kerry, 2004). This characterization of his voting record did not sit well with many voters. The flip-flopping label stuck and he ultimately lost the election.

Consistency and holding to one's values and beliefs is generally valued, and we tend to be wary of people who are inconsistent (Allgeier, 1979). People who are consistent are often lauded for standing up for their principles and following through on their promises. People who are not consistent are often viewed as two-faced and reviled for their deceptiveness.

More importantly, we generally value consistency in our own lives. We usually determine what we should think or do in the future based on what we did in the past (Bem, 1972). We are faced with countless choices every day. It would take a lot of energy to constantly start from scratch and evaluate all the information with which we are faced. It is much easier to start with the assumption that if we did something before, there must have been a good reason and we should probably stick with it.

From a biological standpoint, this makes sense. If I avoided snakes in the past, there was probably a reason. I am not going to question whether snakes are poisonous each and every time I see one. It is much easier to simply always do what I've always done. With more complex issues, however, this can be problematic.

Cognitive dissonance occurs when people hold two or more contradictory values or beliefs or are confronted with new information that conflicts with pre-existing values or beliefs (Festinger, 1957). When this happens people have to either change their original values or beliefs, challenge the newer information, or find a way to make them compatible. Since people generally strive for consistency, it is unlikely for them to change.

Some contemporary examples of this include vaccinations and global warming. There is a belief among many parents that vaccines cause autism. There is no scientific evidence to support this belief (Doja & Roberts, 2006). Since the pre-existing belief and the evidence are not compatible, the only ways to address this cognitive dissonance are to either change the belief or challenge the evidence. Unfortunately, the latter is more common. Researchers found that when these parents were presented with the scientific evidence, they actually became less likely to vaccinate their children (Nyhan, et al., 2014).

Cognitive dissonance has prevented people from accepting the science supporting human contribution to climate change, the safety of genetically modified foods, and the theory of evolution. Time and time again we can see that people are more likely to stick with their pre-existing beliefs, even after being exposed to contradictory evidence (Shtulma & Valcarcel, 2012). It is hard to underestimate the power of consistency.

The question is how can we use this knowledge of consistency and commitment to influence our audience. The first thing to understand is that sometimes, when people are committed against what you are selling, there is not much you can do to change their minds. It is often easier to change what you are pitching than to change people's minds.

Many companies have recognized this and have spent fortunes rebranding themselves and their products. Once public opinion had turned against Phillip Morris for selling cigarettes that killed millions, they changed their name to Altria. When ValuJet got a bad reputation after a couple of plane crashes, they changed their name to AirTran. Because of their involvement in the subprime mortgage crisis, GMAC changed their name to Ally Financial. (Coster, 2009)

These companies realized that the psychological power of consistency was too strong for them to battle. It was easier to start from scratch with a new name than to get people to change their minds. The same holds true for the rest of us. If our pitch is not consistent with our audience's pre-existing values and beliefs, then we need to adjust our focus to be more congruent.

By way of example, let's imagine that you want to persuade an audience that they should do something to protect the environment. You would want to frame the argument differently based on who you are talking to and what they value. If you were talking to people from The Sierra Club, your message would already be consistent with the group's pre-existing values. If you were going to argue the same thing to a group from People for the Ethical Treatment of Animals, or PETA, however, you would naturally frame it differently. If you want to pitch an environmental message and know that they care about animals, it would be better to explain how protecting the environment ties into their pre-existing desire to protect animals. And finally, if you want to pitch an environmental message to a group from the National Rifle Association, or the NRA, you would want to frame it to be consistent with their pre-existing values. You might try to explain how protecting the environment protects hunting grounds.

The key is to not try to change people or challenge their beliefs, but to link your message to what they already believe. Even when your ultimate goal is to change certain parts of people's behavior, it is usually easier to link those changes to pre-existing values and beliefs rather than to start from scratch.

Even when you are not tying into pre-existing values and beliefs, it is possible to increase your chances of influence by creating a pattern of agreement. Rather than waiting until the end of your pitch to seek commitment from your customer or others you are trying to persuade, it can be helpful to get them to agree multiple times as you lead them down the path of persuasion.

The foot in the door technique is a tactic in which people start by asking others to make a small commitment. The theory is that if they make a small commitment first, they are more likely to make a larger one later. By establishing a relationship as well as leading people to be consistent with their past concessions, it is often a very effective tool.

In the 1960s a couple of researchers wanted to see how well this worked, so they conducted two studies. In the first study they asked one set of women if a group of five or six people could come into their homes for two hours and research what kind of products they used. This is obviously an absurd request for anyone. Of the women to whom they made this rather extreme request, only twenty-two percent agreed. With a second set of women, they started by asking them to answer eight brief questions over the phone. Then three days later they asked them to allow a group in their homes for a couple of hours. In this group fifty-three percent agreed to participate.

In the second study they asked people to put a large signs in· their yards that said "Drive Carefully." As before, some of the people had had no prior contact. When faced with such an extreme request, only seventeen percent of this group agreed. Another group had first been asked to put small three-inch signs in their windows. Over fifty-five percent of this group ended up agreeing to the larger sign. (Freedman & Fraser, 1966)

It is hard to underestimate the power of the foot in the door technique. Research has found it successful at getting people to volunteer for a charity (Sherman, 1980), not drive drunk (Taylor & Booth-Butterfield, 1993), get screened for cancer (Taylor & Booth-Butterfield, 1995), and donate their organs (Carducci, et al., 1989). For each of these studies, by starting off with a small commitment, researchers were able to get people to make larger changes that were good for both them and their community.

Hypothetical questions are a wonderful way of starting the chain of agreement without any overt commitment. If you ask people to volunteer, they might say "no." But if you ask them if they think volunteering is important, they will probably say "yes." Then when you ask them if they are going to volunteer, they will feel the need to be consistent with their hypothetical agreement. This can be used for anything. Do you think that eating healthy is important? Are you going to eat healthy? Do you want to get an A in the class? Are you willing to put in the work? If there were a product that could simplify your life, would you want it? Since I am selling that very product, will you buy it?

Surveys, petitions, and pledges can serve the same purpose. Once people have signed a petition in favor of something, they are more likely to take action to support it. Once they indicate a belief in a survey, they are more likely to abide by it. And when people take a public pledge to do something, they are more likely to follow through. When I was in school, we were urged to take pledges not to drink, smoke, or do drugs, to stay in school, and to remain abstinent. As silly as it seemed at the time, these educators and public health professionals were tapping into our innate psychological need for consistency.

The interesting thing is that public commitment is not necessary. Whether other people know someone has committed is not as important as those people knowing that they did personally commit. To prove this, researchers asked a group of residents to commit to conserving more energy and gave them a list of ways to accomplish this. One group was told that because of their willingness to conserve energy, they would have their names published in the newspaper. This group ended up saving more energy. The public commitment to environmentalism was a good motivator. The next month the researchers sent a letter to these people telling them that it would actually not be possible to put their names in the newspaper for conserving energy. The strange thing is that after finding out that they would not be publicized for their environmentalism, these families actually conserved more energy than before. One possible reason for this is that when they were told their names would be publicized, they were doing it only because of external rewards. When that motivation was removed, the remaining reason to save energy was that they were now committed and identified privately as people who would conserve energy. They felt that they should conserve energy because that was the kind of people they were, not because others were judging them. (Pallak, Cook, & Sullivan, 1980)

In the study with "Drive Carefully" signs in people's yards, the researchers actually tried several variations. In addition to starting with the small sign, they also approached some people and asked them to put up a small sign saying "Keep California Beautiful." They asked other people to sign a petition to keep California beautiful. Even though these things had nothing to do with driving carefully, people who agreed to take one of these actions were more likely to put the large "Drive Carefully" sign in their yards. Once they viewed themselves as socially responsible people, they were more likely to participate in other things they thought were socially responsible. It had become part of their self-image.

Even when people are not aware of their commitment, it has an impact on their broader beliefs and decisions. If people commit to being healthy, they are more likely to take steps toward health in general, not just a specific diet or exercise regimen. If they commit to the importance of education, they are likely to take multiple steps toward improving themselves, not just the one you might recommend.

For people who make their living from traditional sales, however, the question is how we can use this power of commitment and consistency to improve the bottom line. If the original commitment and the subsequent call to action do not have to be directly related, this provides an amazing opportunity. Instead of having to start from scratch and make the initial contact, it is possible for the clever sales professional to tap into preexisting commitments. By learning more about your customers you may better harness the power of these commitments. If you know what they are already committed to and how they think of themselves, you will know how better to craft your message and pitch your product or service.

Using Facebook and other social media is a wonderful way of finding out about a person's commitments and self-image. It is also a great way of engaging them. For traditional sales, commitment is gained by making people customers. No matter how small the transaction, they are likely to stick with you. This is one reason that it is so much more expensive to get new customers than it is to keep the ones you have.

With the Internet, however, the foot in the door does not have to be a sale. Getting people to "like" a Facebook page is a commitment. Getting them to sign up for your email list is a commitment. Getting them to take action online is a commitment. And once people have made that commitment, they are far more likely to purchase. Establishing a relationship is an important step that is often overlooked by those who simply want to jump to the sale.

Authority

Respect for authority is universal. All cultures, to some degree, teach people to defer to those with more power or expertise. Even though America is fairly egalitarian, respect for elders is still deeply engrained in our culture. See the extra section on culture at the end of this book for more information on respect for authority in various world cultures.

Every major world religion teaches respect for authority. The Judeo-Christian scriptures start with an allegory about respect for authority. In the book of Genesis Eve ignored God's command and by eating a piece of fruit she doomed all of humanity (Genesis 3). God instructed Abraham to sacrifice his son Isaac as a test of his faith (Genesis 22). The message of respect for God's authority is clear.

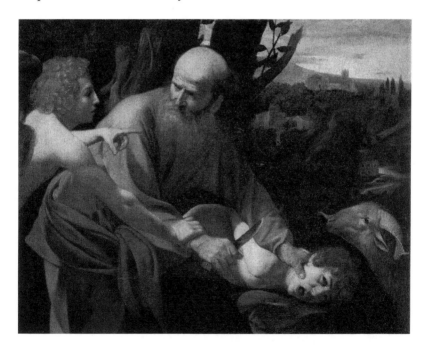

From an evolutionary perspective, authority serves a useful purpose. According to Richard Dawkins (2006):

More than any other species, we survive by the accumulated experience of previous generations, and that experience needs to be passed on to children for their protection and well-being. Theoretically, children might learn from personal experience not to go too near a cliff edge, not to eat untried red berries, not to swim in crocodile-infested waters. But, to say the least, there will be a selective advantage to child brains that possess the rule of thumb: believe, without question, whatever your grown-ups tell you. Obey your parents; obey the tribal elders, especially when they adopt a solemn, minatory tone. Trust your elders without question.

Regardless of why people are so likely to defer to authority, it is clear that it has a huge impact on us. It is also clear that it is an important element of the process of influence.

Yale psychologist Stanley Milgram conducted one of the best known pieces of research on respect for authority (1963). Following the trial of Nazi war criminal Adolf Eichmann, who had claimed he was "just following orders" (Cesarani, 2005), Miller wanted to see if there was something unique about Germans that made them more obedient to authority figures. What he found was that most anyone can be susceptible to undue influence from those in power.

In the experiment Milgram asked for volunteers to participate in a study about memory. When they came into the lab, they were randomly labeled either a "learner" or a "teacher." The learner was taken into another room, strapped into a chair, and connected to electrodes. The researcher told the teacher that he would be giving the learner a list of words to remember. The teacher would then test the learner and be responsible for remotely administering a shock every time he got the wrong answer, with each successive shock getting stronger. The learner said that he had a heart condition, but the teacher was assured that, even though the shock would hurt, there would be no long-term damage. The teacher was even allowed to feel the initial 15-volt shock.

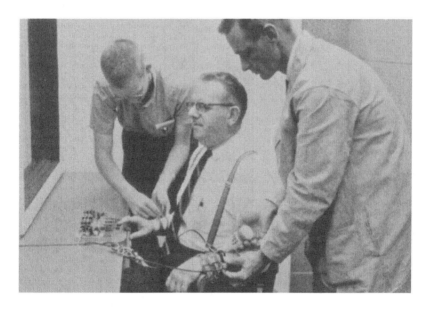

As the experiment proceeded and the learner got answers wrong, the researcher instructed the teacher to press a button and administer a shock. As things progressed, the teacher could hear the learner screaming in pain and asking to stop the test. The teachers generally wanted to stop, but were urged to continue by the researcher. Even though they were generally sweating, trembling, and stuttering, 65% of them proceeded to administer the shock of 450-volts.

As you might have guessed, the learner was in on it and was never actually shocked. The purpose of the experiment was to see what the teacher would do when ordered by someone in a position of authority to hurt another person. As Milgram (1974) put it:

> Stark authority was pitted against the subjects' strongest moral imperatives against hurting others, and, with the subjects' ears ringing with the screams of the victims, authority won more often than not. The extreme willingness of adults to go to almost any lengths on the command of an authority constitutes the chief finding of the study and the fact most urgently demanding explanation.

Hopefully, we would all use our authority for far more noble purposes, but it is hard to deny the fact that authority is a hugely powerful component of influence.

There are a few key things that give us authority or take it away. We have more control over some components of authority than others. Titles and credentials are the result of hard work. Height and age are the result of genetics and time. Clothing and attitude are generally under our control.

Titles and credentials are one of the most direct ways to establish credibility. Honorifics, such as "Dr.," "professor," "officer," "your honor," "captain," "reverend," or "father" automatically give people authority. In order to receive these titles, people generally have to go through extensive training or pass comprehensive exams. We are conditioned to believe that these people are more knowledgeable, more honest, and more deserving of respect. Slogans like "Four out of five dentists recommend…" have helped Trident sell gum. Respect for those titles is so strong that it even works for those whose titles are not actually real. Actor Peter Bergman famously said, "I am not a doctor, but I play one on TV," to sell Vicks.

These honorifics are useful shortcuts in determining whom we should trust. The problem is that very few people check their validity and they can be very easy to fake. You can become an ordained minister through the Universal Life Church for $30. You can get a "life experience doctorate" for a few hundred dollars with no classes or dissertation needed. If you have actual credentials, however, this is a wonderful way of establishing your authority.

There is not much we can do to control how tall we are, but being taller does make us seem more authoritative (Blaker, 2013). CEOs are taller than the general public and people who are taller make more money (Feintzeig, 2014). In the majority of presidential elections in the United States since 1900, the taller candidate won the election, and presidents are generally taller than the average person (Stulp, 2013).

Being older, taller, and more imposing makes people seem more authoritative. When I was younger, I once grew a beard to make myself seem older for a job interview. I got the job. A female friend of mine once dyed her hair gray so she would seem more mature while doing rounds at the hospital. She found that patients took her more seriously.

Clothing and specific uniforms often denote authority and are much easier to control. Military insignia show what rank officers and enlisted men and women have. Doctors wear long white coats, residents wear medium length white coats, and medical students are relegated to short white coats. The rank of people in a restaurant kitchen can often be determined by looking at the height of their hats. The head chef will have the highest hat.

People tend to automatically genuflect before those in uniform. In one piece of research, someone in a security guard uniform asked people on the street to do various things. They also made the same requests while dressed in street clothes. People were more likely to comply when the person asking was in uniform. (Bickman, 1974) People rated police officers as being more honest, helpful, and good when they were in uniform than when they were wearing regular clothes (Mauro, 1984).

We are conditioned to trust and obey those dressed in uniform. Even the *uniform* of business people, a suit or pantsuit, denotes authority. In one study researchers had a man jaywalk, crossing an intersection through traffic. Half the time he was wearing a suit and tie. Half the time he was wearing casual clothing. They found that 3.5 times as many people followed the man when he was dressed formally. (Lefkowitz, Blake, & Mouton, 1955)

This last study shows how automatic our respect for uniforms and those in power is. While there might be a reason to assume that people should listen to a security guard or trust a police officer, there is no reason to assume that a businessman is any less likely to be hit by oncoming traffic. If you want to build authority, clothing is one of the easiest ways. The question, as we discussed in the section about liking, is whether dressing differently is worth the risk of differentiating yourself from the people you are trying to influence.

The final way to establish authority is with attitude. As simple as it sounds, by simply speaking with authority and sounding like you know what you are talking about, people are likely to listen to you. If you can present your message with an air of confidence, your customers are apt to listen.

Likability

It should not come as a surprise to learn that people are more likely to listen to people they like, more likely to help people they like, and more likely to actually buy from people they like. As we move toward a standardization of products and services in many fields, the deciding factor when choosing with whom to do business is who the customer likes the most. Mass produced items are the same no matter who sells them. Highly regulated services, like insurance, are all basically the same.

While there are differences in teaching ability and medical care, all doctors have to follow the standard of care and all teachers have to follow the standard curriculum. The major difference is whether or not the customers, clients, patients, or students like the person they are dealing with. If you can get people to like you, the battle is half won.

A prime example of liking being used to facilitate sales is Tupperware parties. Brownie Wise created these ingenious parties for Tupperware in the early 1950s (Bax, 2010). Instead of going to an impersonal showroom, women are invited to a friend's house. Even though there may be a professional salesperson there, the real request to buy is coming from a friend. Regardless of who actually takes the order, everyone knows that they are helping their friend make a commission.

Research shows that the strength of the relationship between the host and the guests is twice as likely to determine what products people buy as an actual preference for one product or another (Frenzen & Davis, 1990). There are party games and free gifts that help make everyone feel comfortable and encourage socializing. This, combined with the obligation of friendship, motivates people to buy things (Taylor, 1978). It is easy to walk past a plastic bowl at the store or even turn down a stranger, but when a friend asks, our natural defenses are down.

Thanks to the success of Tupperware parties, many other companies have adopted this business model. Pampered Chef and Princess House sell kitchenware, Cookie Lee sells jewelry, and Passion parties sell sex toys. There is no shortage of products to buy and no shortage of people you like trying to sell them to you.

Another great example of liking leading to influence would be Oprah Winfrey. Her media empire revolves around her very friendly persona. Millions of women consume her content because they like her. And companies have sold hundreds of millions of dollars worth of products just because Oprah mentioned it.

An article in Inc. Magazine discussed this phenomenon:

> The so-called 'Oprah Effect' can bring fame to an obscure company translating into

dramatically increased sales. Even a casual mention of a product, exposed to her 44 million weekly viewers, is a boon for the company that makes or sells that product. (Hornbuckle, 2009)

When she added books to *Oprah's Book Club*, they invariably became best sellers. And when she included products in her annual list of *Oprah's Favorite Things,* the companies that sold them saw their sales take off.

People did not value Oprah's opinion because she was an authority, but because she was likeable. She comes across as the friend every woman wishes she had, and thanks to the power of television, they do.

Oprah's power to influence does not end with books and home products. In 2007 she endorsed Barack Obama in the Democratic Primary. During Oprah's campaign appearances with Obama, she drew the largest crowds of the campaign season, topping out at over 33,000 people at an event in South Carolina (Hamby & Malveaux, 2007). Economists researching

Oprah's impact on the election estimate that she contributed to just over a million votes for Obama and led to Obama's victory. According to Craig Garthwaite, one of the researchers, "It does appear to have been a decisive, if not a deciding, factor" (Garthwaite & Moore, 2008). It is hard to underestimate the power of likability.

So the question that haunted many of us on the first day of school remains. How do we get people to like us? In addition to just being an all around nice person, there are a few keys to increase likability. They are physical attractiveness, similarity, contact, compliments (Cialdini, 2009) and reciprocity.

It should come as no surprise that people generally like physically attractive people more than others. Teachers are more likely to view attractive children as more intelligent than their less attractive classmates (Ritts, Patterson, & Tubbs, 1992). Employers are more likely to hire people that are more attractive (Mack & Rainey, 1990). And when they are hired, attractive people earn an average of 12%-14% more than their unattractive coworkers (Hammermesh & Biddle, 1994). Voters are more likely to vote for people who are more attractive (Budesheim & DePaola, 1994). And attractive criminals are twice as likely to avoid jail as their unattractive counterparts (Stweart, 1980).

Research shows that we are more likely to be persuaded by attractive people (Chaiken, 1979) and more likely to help attractive people in need (Benson, Karabenic, & Lerner, 1976). In spite of this overarching bias toward more attractive people, we are generally unaware of it. This bias toward beauty often operates at an unconscious level as we make split second judgments about others based on their attractiveness (Olson & Marshuetz, 2005). We assume that if someone is attractive, he or she must be good. This sense is instilled from an early age. In children's cartoons and fairy tales, the heroes and heroines are attractive while the villains are ugly. Snow White was the "fairest of all" while the evil queen was ugly.

I would obviously not suggest that people get plastic surgery in order to influence others or increase sales, but it is hard to deny that physical attractiveness makes a difference. There are things that can be done to help overcome this unconscious bias and have a more positive influence on those around us. As clichéd as it might sound, dress for success. We do not have control over our genes, but with a consistent focus on style and grooming we can make ourselves look better and enhance our influence. As Mark Twain said, "Clothes make the man. Naked people have little or no influence on society."

Dressing well is important, but it is equally important not to go overboard. If we dress too formally we run the risk of interfering with the second key to liking, similarity. As a general rule, we like people who are similar to us (Burger et al., 2004). People feel a natural affinity for people they have something in common with. It could be elements that we have very little control over, such as culture, race, or background. Or it could be personal things such as our religion, politics, or personality traits. People are likely to feel a sense of commonality with people who dress in a similar way.

I attended a sales training meeting where the speaker spent an exorbitant amount of time instructing us on the finer points of fashion. He insisted that in order to be successful we needed to dress to the nines. If the goal is to establish authority, that makes perfect sense. The problem is that it is unlikely to establish similarity. I do not generally walk around wearing a three-piece suit nor do most of the people I know.

It is typically better to dress like the people you want to persuade, but a step up. Dressing a little nicer gives you authority and shows that you are taking the interaction seriously, but dressing close to their level shows that you have something in common. Research shows that people are more likely to give money to those who dress like them (Emswiller, Deaux, & Willits, 1971). It has also been found that people are more likely to buy from a salesperson of a similar age, religion, and political affiliation. (Evans, 1963).

Armed with the cold reading skills we covered earlier, it should not be very hard to glean quite a bit about the people you are dealing with. Based on this knowledge, less ethical people might be tempted to fake similarities to facilitate liking. If the person you are dealing with loves the Broncos, so do you. If he is religious, so are you. If she grew up in Milwaukee, so did you.

But this really is not necessary. Despite our many differences, we invariably still have quite a bit in common. With the countless aspects of your life, some of them are bound to line up with the person you are dealing with. Do you both have kids? Do you both worry about the future? Do you both value hard work? No matter how different you are from someone else, there are sure to be some similarities to draw on. Authentic similarities are always better than forced or fabricated ones.

Even something as simple as mirroring someone can help establish similarity. In addition to helping you get inside their heads and understand what they are thinking and feeling, mirroring unconsciously shows others that you are similar. If they are feeling excited and they see you are as well, you have something in common. We have a natural habit of mirroring others. By making use of it, establishing similarity and being likeable will be easy.

We generally like people and things that we are familiar with (Monahan, Murphy, & Zajonc, 2000). Simply spending time with people, or having exposure to them, makes us like them more. This influence is often unconscious, but has a huge impact on our affinity for others.

In one study participants were shown pictures of people's faces on a screen. The images were flashed so fast that they could not remember having seen them. When they met the people in the pictures and were asked to rank how much they liked them, the participants ended up liking those they had seen more. Because liking leads to influence, they were more likely to be persuaded by those people's statements (Bornstein, Leone, & Gallery, 1987).

Research has found that people are more likely to vote for candidates they are familiar with. Some voters actually choose the candidate whose name sounds more familiar, even if they do not know anything about their policies (Grush, McKeough, & Ahlering, 1978). They are also more likely to like brands and products that they have more exposure to. In a study of online advertising, researchers showed banner advertisements for a product. Even though they did not realize they had seen the ads, participants that had been exposed to more ads for the product reported that they liked the product more than those that had seen few or no ads (Fang, Singh, & Ahulwailia, 2007). Even though we may ignore the barrage of online ads we see, they still have an impact on us. The more we are exposed to them, the more likely we are to like them, whether we realize it or not.

Perhaps the best example of this is *The Pepsi Challenge* from the early 1980s. Pepsi began doing blind taste tests where they asked people to try a sip of Pepsi and a sip of Coke. It turned out that based only on taste, people preferred Pepsi over Coke. This was not just a publicity stunt. When Coke conducted the same test, they found the same thing. In Coke's own study people preferred Pepsi 57% to 43%.

To address this problem, Coke's chemists adjusted the recipe to make their soda sweeter. In a blind taste test this soda beat Pepsi by 6% to 8%. In 1985 this new formula was released as *New Coke*. Logically, since more people like the taste of Pepsi and New Coke, one would expect those two drinks to sell better. That is not, however, what happened. (Yglesias, 2013)

There was a customer revolt against *New Coke*. The company received over 400,000 calls and letters of complaint from people that wanted the original Coke back (Hays, 2005). The company re-released the original soda as *Coke Classic* and eventually discontinued New Coke. To this day the original Coke outsells Pepsi by roughly two-to-one (US Beverage Results, 2014). The question (often dubbed the *Pepsi Paradox*) is, why would twice as many people drink something that doesn't taste as good as the alternative? The answer lies in branding, familiarity, and liking.

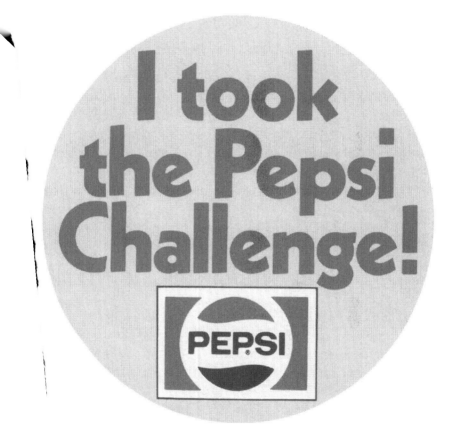

It turns out that many people would prefer to have something they are familiar with and already like. Pepsi's slogan was "Let your taste decide," but research indicates that taste was not the deciding factor. In one study participants were hooked up to an fMRI to measure brain activity while they tried different sodas. In a blind taste test, most participants preferred Pepsi and those that did showed a higher level of activity in the ventral putamen, one of the brain's pleasure centers. When participants were told what they were drinking and given a Coke or a Pepsi, there was increased activity in the medial prefrontal cortex, an area of the brain associated with thinking and judging (McClure, et al. (2004.)

When it comes to soft drinks, brand recognition is more important than taste. When it comes to those of us working to influence others, familiarity is one of our greatest tools. There is no shortcut to putting in the time to be sure our customers know who we are and enjoy being around us.

Another guideline, when it comes to liking, is that people generally like people who like them. Compliments are great ways of establishing liking. We all like to be around those who say nice things and are less likely to stay around those who say negative things.

Research shows that praise really does work in getting others to like us. In one study men interacted with people who needed a favor from them. In one group they received only compliments. In another group they were criticized. And in the third group they got both positive and negative comments. The researchers found three things. As would be expected, the men liked those who praised them the most. A little less obviously, this preference held true even though they knew the people praising them needed a favor from them and stood to benefit if they were liked. Somewhat surprisingly, it did not matter whether or not these compliments were honest. (Drachman deCarufel, & Insko, 1978)

I am sure we have all had this experience. When people want something from us, they often compliment us. "You are so good at that… Would you mind helping me with it?" Even though we know exactly what is happening, it still works.

As an additional note, one of the most effective compliments is remembering a person's name. Something

120

simple as remembering people's names and referring to them by name can have a big impact on liking and influence. Research shows that customers viewed name remembrance as a compliment and increased their likelihood of complying with a purchase request (Howard, Gengler, & Jain, 1995).

The final thing that gets people to like us is doing something for them. "I owe you one" is a ubiquitous phrase that perfectly represents the idea of reciprocity. Whether we realize it or not, this common sentiment is integral to civilized society and has helped humans thrive. Reciprocity can explain altruism and justice. Reciprocity refers to the general rule that people repay kind words and actions with the same or often times better. Likewise, they repay unkind words and actions with the same or even worse (Fehr & Gächter, 2000).

Humans have evolved to like people who do things for them and to value reciprocity. The basic principle is that if I help you now, you will be more likely to help me in the future. This is of great value to a species trying to survive in a dangerous world (Aronson, Wilson, & Akert, 2012). After all, none of us live in a bubble, and if those around us survive and prosper, our chances of surviving and prospering are greatly enhanced. This concept of indebtedness and reciprocity allowed humans to have a division of labor, to trade goods and services, and ultimately to prosper as a community (Ridley, 1997).

Because of this community focus, the reciprocity does not always need to be directed back toward the giver (Trivers, 1971). Altruism is when we selflessly show concern for the well being of others. This is a highly prized trait in most cultures. If you are willing to help others when they are in need, you are more likely to help me when I am in need. Therefore, I will help you when you are in need so that you are around to help me and others when we are in need.

A perfect example of this is the idea of paying it forward. By having the beneficiary of a good deed pay back his or her debt by rendering a good deed to others, the theory is that we can make the world a better place for all of us. There are countless examples of this kind of altruism, but a very concise and highly publicized example took place at Starbucks in August of 2014. A woman at a drive-thru in Saint Petersburg, Florida, ordered her drink and said that she would like to pay for the drink of the person in line behind her. The next person decided to pay it forward and pay for the next person's drink.

This happened time after time until Peter Schorsch, person number 458 in the pay it forward line, drove up to the window. He refused to pay it forward saying that he "had to put an end to it." Headlines called him a "Jerk," a "Curmudgeon," and even a "Cheap Bastard," (Caesar, 2014; Wagner, 2014; Chan, 2014). He felt compelled to come out publicly and tell people that he was not a Grinch and claim that he left a $100 tip for the barista.

Schorsch serves as a poster boy for what happens when people refuse to reciprocate. We value those that reciprocate positive actions and generally despise those that do not (Wedekind & Milinski, 2000). Those that do not honor their debts to others, whether they asked for them or not, are often called "moochers," "freeloaders," or worse.

To test the power of reciprocity, Dennis Regan (1971), a psychologist at Cornell University, invited subjects to participate in what they were told was an art appreciation experiment. They were paired with another volunteer, who was actually a research assistant. They would always take a two-minute break. Half the time the confederate would come back and tell the volunteer he got a soda for himself and went ahead and brought one for him as well. The other times the confederate came back empty handed.

At the end of the experiment the confederate told the volunteer that he was selling raffle tickets for a new car and that he would win a prize if he sold the most tickets. He then asked the volunteer if he would buy some of the tickets. In the cases where the confederate had brought back a soda, the volunteers bought an average of twice as many tickets. It did not matter that the volunteer did not ask for the soda or that the soda was a very inexpensive gift. The mere act of giving a nominal gift actually increased the likelihood of compliance.

After the experiment, the volunteers were also asked to rate how likeable the other person was. In the control group there was a correlation between how much the volunteers liked the confederate and how many raffle tickets they bought. What is surprising is that the confederate bringing the volunteer a gift, in this case a soda, completely wiped away the influence of likeability. It did not matter whether or not the volunteers actually liked the confederate. When he gave them a gift, they felt indebted to him and experienced an overwhelming urge to comply with his request. This bit of information should come as a relief for people with a repugnant personality. No matter how unlikeable you are, there is still hope. All it costs is the price of a soda.

Perhaps one of the most widely publicized and despised forms of reciprocity is the one that occurs between politicians and lobbyists. A quid pro quo arrangement where lobbyists pay for specific legislation is considered bribery and is against the law. It is impossible, however, to outlaw the human inclination to reciprocate. Lobbyists, and the organizations that hire them, count on the fact that the politicians they support will feel indebted to them and will feel compelled to repay that debt by crafting legislation that will benefit them.

The Sunlight Foundation analyzed the top 200 most politically active corporations. They found that between 2007 and 2012 they spent a combined total of $5.8 billion on federal lobbying and campaign contributions in the United States. That sounds like a lot of money until you learn that those same corporations received $4.4 trillion dollars in business and support from the federal government. (Allison & Harkins, 2014) When put in that perspective, this money seems like a great investment.

What If Our Presidential Candidates Were NASCAR Drivers?

Top contributors to both candidates' campaigns based on donors' employers.

U.S.News & WORLD REPORT Photo Credit: Photo Works / Maria Dryfhout / Spirit of America / Shutterstock.com
Source: **Center For Responsive Politics**

Virtually everyone not working in politics agrees that lobbying tends to distort the political process. A somewhat more ambiguous example, however, might be doctors and their uneasy relationship with pharmaceutical companies. It is estimated that pharmaceutical companies spend an average of between $8,000 and $13,000 per year on each physician. These can range from thousands of dollars at a time for speaking fees or travel, to small gifts, samples, and meals.

Doctors do not generally believe that these gifts influence the course of treatment they recommend. Research, however, tells a different story. It turns out that doctors who receive gifts from pharmaceutical companies, even in very small amounts, are more likely to prescribe their medications (Wazana, 2000). This type of reciprocity may be good for pharmaceutical companies' bottom lines, but it is not necessarily in the best interest of patients.

In a somewhat less dramatic example of the use of social proof, researchers looked at the relationship between giving candy to restaurant patrons and the size of the tip they left. They found that in the control group, without candy, patrons left a tip of about 15%. The average tip size, when the waiters brought a piece of candy for everyone along with the bill, was almost 18%. (Strohmetz, 2002)

Reciprocity is a wonderful investment. There is a tire shop near my house that offers free tire repairs. The last time I got a flat tire, I went to them and they quickly fixed it. There were no strings attached. It didn't matter where I originally bought the tires. And they did not try to get me to buy new tires. They just patched the hole and I went on my way. This ended up being a great way of getting business. The next time I needed tires, I felt like I owed them my business. But since their prices are higher, the next time I got a flat tire, I went elsewhere and paid to have it fixed. It was cheaper to pay for the repair than to feel that I owed them my business the next time I needed tires.

Many businesses recognize the power of reciprocity. Inc. Magazine wrote a profile of Good Catalog Company and how the owner used reciprocity to increase sales.

> She selects gifts from leftover inventory or product samples and ships them with a personalized letter. The average gift has a $50 retail value but is worth only about $15 at the warehouse sale, at which Todd would otherwise sell it. The freebie works wonders, according to Todd. Within a few months of starting the program, she says, the gift recipients' response rates to mailings rose from 5% to 25%, while

their average purchase rose from $100 to $300. (Gruner, 1996)

There are countless examples of reciprocity at work. Stores regularly give out free samples. Many charities send direct mail with a nominal gift, because it increases the response rate. The American Disabled Veterans organization found that they got an 18% response rate with their normal mailer. When they included a free, unsolicited gift of personalized address labels, however, their response rate went up to 35% (Cialdini, 2009). Many in the direct mail industry have discovered the power of gifts. I have received labels, refrigerator magnets, and even books to encourage me to reciprocate.

For this to work, however, there are two important points to keep in mind. First, it must not be considered a payment for services rendered or a sale. People tend to reciprocate with more than the value of the gift as long as the giver does not ask for, or "suggest," a specific amount. Secondly, the gift or favor should be framed as being valuable. This may mean that it is expensive or that it is personal and exclusive.

The personalized mailing labels only cost a few cents. If the recipients saw this as a direct exchange of money, then their donations would only be a few cents. But the recipients are not buying the labels (that they probably did not want in the first place). Instead, they are responding to this gift with a gift of their own. It is safe to say that this second gift will be far more expensive than the initial one.

The gift should also seem valuable. In the case of the labels, they may not have monetary value, but they are personalized with the recipient's name. If it is not personalized, then establishing an actual value can be helpful. If people see the gift as being worthless, then there is no need to reciprocate. If you are going to give people a book, do not give them a free book. Give them a $20 book for free.

The reason Jehovah's Witnesses cannot make use of reciprocity as they give out *The Watchtower* is that people know that they are always given out for free and, therefore, have no monetary value. If they were to say that each magazine costs $5.00, but that it was a special gift, it might have more of an impact.

In the tipping experiment we discussed earlier, the waiters were able to increase their average tips 3% by providing a few cents worth of candy. The best results were achieved, however, when the waiter would give people a piece of candy and then start to walk away, then turn around and offer another piece of candy as an afterthought. (Strohmetz, 2002) By taking this simple action they were making the candy seem more valuable. If they give a piece of candy to everyone automatically, because it is part of the restaurant policy, it does not seem as valuable. If they come back and decide to give an extra piece, it seems more exclusive and therefore more valuable.

Next time you are trying to influence people, ask yourself what you are giving them. How are you being of service to them? How are you making their lives better? As you can see, a gift can often be one of the strongest sales tools. If you can get people to like you, the rest is a piece of cake.

Exclusivity

There is a private club in the Hollywood Hills. It is in a hundred-year-old mansion with secret passages and hidden rooms. There are magicians roaming the club and rumors of ghosts. There is a strict dress code and you have to be at least twenty-one to visit in the evening. Most importantly, the only way to get in is to be invited by a member. From the first time I heard of this amazing club, I knew I had to go to the Magic Castle.

Luckily, my father knew someone who knew someone who could get me one of the coveted invitations. I went there with some friends to celebrate my twenty first birthday. It was one of the most amazing experiences of my life. Years later I would become a member and perform my mind reading show on stage at the Magic Castle.

Club 33 is a private club at Disneyland. The entrance is a non-descript green door in New Orleans Square. To be admitted you must press the intercom button and confirm that you have a reservation. Club 33 is notorious for having the longest line in a park known for long lines. There is a fourteen-year waiting list to become a member. If accepted, there is a $25,000 initiation fee and $10,000 in annual dues (Michaelson, 2012).

I would offer more details about Club 33, but I have never been there. This bothers me immensely. I have visited Disneyland countess times and have ridden on every ride, seen every show, and eaten at every restaurant. I do not, however, know anyone who can get me into Club 33. Going to the Magic Castle is fun for me, but Club 33 is unattainable and, therefore, even more valuable.

We generally want what we can't have. We are programmed to think that if something is exclusive, it must be more valuable. From an economic standpoint, when demand outpaces supply, the resources become more valuable. From a psychological standpoint, when someone tells us we cannot have something, we generally want it more. Since things that are better are usually more difficult to get, we assume that if it is difficult it get, it must be better (Lynn, 1989).

We are going to look at examples ranging from gemstones to fine art, from Barbra Streisand to banned books, and from Disney cartoons to a slapstick comedy. But let's start with something everyone can appreciate, cookies. Researchers wanted to see whether the abundance of cookies impacted people's perception of how good they were. They gave half the study participants a jar with two cookies in it and the other half got a jar with ten cookies. As you might expect, the group that had the jar with fewer cookies thought they were better.

In a second experiment they had people start out with a jar full of ten cookies. Then, before they had a chance to try one, a researcher took eight of them away. Half of the people were told that the cookies were being taken because there was an accident and they were running low on cookies. In the other half, they were told that they were being taken away because of an increase in demand. Even though all of the cookies were exactly the same, the ones in the latter group were rated as being the best of all. By combining scarcity and social proof the researchers actually made cookies taste better. (Worchel, Lee, & Adewole, 1975)

We are hard wired to believe that scarce and exclusive things are valuable and gemstones have historically been one of the most difficult things to get. If you ask jewelers what makes a diamond valuable, they will probably tell you it is the four Cs: carat, clarity, color, and cut. If you ask a psychologist or an economist, however, they will certainly tell you it is the rarity. What makes these shiny rocks worth more than cubic zirconia is that there are far fewer of them in circulation. As with most products, this does not happen by chance. De Beers, the diamond cartel, keeps a tight control of the majority of the world's diamond supply. By keeping diamonds scarce and slowly releasing the supply, they have been able to keep diamond prices high for decades (Kanfer, 1995).

All collectibles, from baseball cards to fine art, derive their value in large part from their scarcity. The fewer copies there are of a comic book, the more valuable it is. And the harder it is to acquire a piece of art, the more people are willing to pay to get it. Paul Cézanne painted five versions of The Card Players in 1894-1895. In 2012 The Qatari royal family purchased one of the paintings for $250,000,000 (Peers, 2012) Unlike more tangible products, however, in the digital age most art is available to the public. You are able to enjoy the picture below for the price of this book. The difference, however, is that while there can be infinite copies of this painting, there is only one original of this specific painting.

Scarcity, or implied scarcity, is a great way of influencing people's desires and actions. Leading marketing and sales professionals have found many ways of harnessing the power of scarcity. Stores often keep very limited numbers of products on the showroom floor, which makes their salespeople trek back and forth to the storeroom more often. This creates an implied scarcity. Having an abundant supply of products sometimes makes people want them less (Schwarz, 1984).

If there is a large selection, the consumer has the power to decide whether or not to buy one of the many products on display. If there is only a floor model that is not for sale, the seller has the power. Some salespeople get the customer to commit to the purchase before searching for it. Simply asking the customer if he or she will take the product if there is one is a very effective tactic. Even when no commitment is requested, the theory of reciprocity dictates that people are more likely to purchase if the salesperson has gone to all the work of searching for a product.

Many companies work hard to keep up the appearance of scarcity and make their products seem exclusive. Some retailers would rather destroy excess inventory than donate it to charities, because having too many products floating around makes them less exclusive and, therefore, worth less (Dwyer, 2012). Even if the products are not scarce, it is important to create that impression. Infomercials often include calls to action such as "act now, supplies are limited" or "call while supplies last." Amazon.com sometimes includes warnings on product listings that tell people, "Only 3 left in stock - order soon."

Marketers often issue limited editions of collector's items in order to create scarcity. Disney does a wonderful job of this with the Disney Vault. Instead of leaving their animated films on the market, they regularly take them off the market and re-release them a few years later. They make them available for a limited time and then put them on moratorium. Without this, the prices would slowly drop over time. By limiting their release to every few years, effectively keeping them scarce, Disney has kept the prices higher.

In addition to scarcity because of limited numbers, we also have scarcity based on limited time and even censorship. Sales and limited time offers are wonderful ways of getting people to take action. If they are in danger of losing out on something, they are more likely to take action.

Sometimes things are exclusive because they are censored and only certain people have the right to have them. Throughout the ages various governments, school boards, and even Barbra Streisand, have tried to censor information. These attempts are often doomed to failure, because there are few better ways of getting people to want something, especially information, than to tell them they can't have it (Worchel, 1992). There is no better way to get students to read a book than to tell them they can't read it. In one study a group of

133

students were shown an advertisement for a book with a warning that said, "a book for adults only, restricted to those 21 years and over." Another group was shown the same advertisement with no warning. They found that the group that saw the warning liked the book more and were more excited about reading it (Zellinger et al., 1974).

Barbra Streisand learned firsthand that censorship does not work in 2003. A photographer took over 12,000 pictures of the California coast and posted them on a website. One of those pictures was of Barbra Streisand's house. She filed a lawsuit to have the picture removed from the website. Once that fact was publicized, lots of people wanted to see what she was trying to censor. Before she called attention to the picture, only a few people had viewed it online. In the month after her lawsuit, over 420,000 people looked at it (Rogers, 2003). This has been dubbed the "Streisand Effect" (Masnick, 2005).

North Korea demonstrated the power of the Streisand Effect on a much larger scale. Sony Pictures produced a Seth Rogan comedy called *The Interview*. In the movie the CIA sent Rogan and James Franco to North Korea to assassinate supreme leader Kim Jong-un. North Korea demanded that Sony not release the film. They hacked into the company's servers and threatened to attack any theaters that screened the film. This subpar, sophomoric comedy would likely have been overlooked by most of the public. When Sony initially capitulated and pulled the film, however, the public clamored to see the now scarce movie. North Korea's attempt at censorship was the best thing that could have happened to *The Interview*.

For environmental reasons, in 2014 the United States phased out certain types of incandescent light bulbs in favor of more efficient types. As a result of finding out that they were going to be banned, 30% of people surveyed said that they planned to stockpile them (Osram, 2013). Finding out that people want certain kinds of light bulbs more when they are outlawed sheds light on the results of attempts to prohibit certain kinds of drugs, alcohol, and even junk food.

It can also shed light on a particularly effective method of influence. Countless marketers have used the assertion that they are going to tell you something that you aren't supposed to know. "Find out what the government doesn't want you to know." "Read the report *ABC Company* tried to censor." "Find out what your doctor isn't telling you." If students are more likely to read a book they aren't supposed to, why not get adults to clamor for a message they think someone is trying to hide from them. People do not like to miss out on things.

FOMO, or the fear of missing out, is becoming more common as we are bombarded with more and more information (Przybylski et al, 2013). Those of us addicted to the Internet and our smart phones know this feeling all too well. When new information is available, we must find out what it is. If someone calls me, even when I am talking with someone else, I feel the need to answer the call. I have a limited amount of time to answer the phone and if I do not act before the last ring, I will lose out on finding out what my friend, or more likely a telemarketer, has to say.

This fear of running out of time is used to great effect by some marketers. The point of sales and other limited time offers is to get us to take action quickly before we run out of time. Salespeople often tell prospective customers that there is a limited time offer and if they do not buy now, the prices will probably go up. eBay listings have a countdown clock and if you don't bid in time, you are likely to miss out on the product. Of course, there are many other products on eBay, salespeople will generally give you the same prices later, and there will always be another sale. But we are wired to worry that we might miss out if we don't act now.

In our service economy time is often the scarcest commodity. As many motivational speakers are fond of reminding us, we each have 84,600 seconds per day. We need to figure out what we do with that time. For those of us who traffic in information, our time is our greatest asset. And the time we give others is of great value.

As a teacher, the main thing I have to offer is my time in the classroom and the time I meet with my students. Therapists offer their time counseling people about their lives. Lawyers offer their time counseling people about their transgressions. And though medical professionals do actual tests and procedures, much of the time is spent simply talking to patients and diagnosing their conditions.

The question is, for those of us who monetize our time, how do we create scarcity and exclusivity? We often find ourselves having countless repetitive interactions with different people, where we dispense very similar information. I have given the same lectures countless times and everyday I answer the same questions with the same answers. I never really realized the repetitiveness until I asked a rhetorical question in class and then proceeded to answer it myself. One of my students started laughing. I asked what was so funny and she pointed out that it sounded like I was following a script and had said the same thing a hundred times. She was right.

I realized that I was not making our group interaction seem exclusive. The class was not special. It was an experience they could have in any one of my other classes. From then on I focused on making all of my experiences seem special and unique. Even if I have said something before to another class or another student, I try to make it sound as though it is the first time. Since my time is the most exclusive of all resources, I want each and every one of them to feel that they got something special from me.

Method of Influence

Now that you have a solid understanding of the keys to influence, let's move on to the method of influence. While the keys to influence are crucial in making a connection with people and moving them, the method of influence section offers step-by-step instructions. There are five steps to persuading people to take action.

Alan Monroe, of Purdue University, developed what he called Monroe's Motivated Sequence in the 1930s. It has been seen as one of the most effective models for influencing people. When you follow his five simple steps, you start by getting the audience's attention. You then help them see that they have an unmet need and offer a way of satisfying it. After that you motivate your audience by helping them visualize the results. And finally, you offer a call to action to get them to do what you want.

In this chapter, we will cover each section in the influence process with research on how the steps work, suggestions on how to implement them, and examples to show how others have used them. Understanding the essential parts of the persuasive process will make it easier to shape the interaction and achieve your goal.

Step 1: Attention

The first step in the persuasion process is getting the attention of your audience members. If you can't get them interested in what you have to say, the rest of your interaction will be pointless. You need to make them want to listen to you and find out more about your product or service. If you do a good job getting their attention, you will not be forcing your message on them, but will be giving them information they will actually be open to.

If you have a captive audience, this process is much easier. If you work in the medical field and the patient made an appointment to see you, you will probably have his or her attention. In my classes the students have to be there if they want to be marked present and they have to pay attention if they want to pass the test.

If you are the one who initiated contact, it will naturally take a little more work to get a person interested. When people seek out a doctor or sign up for a college course, they have already signaled their interest. If you are cold calling a prospective customer, you had better get their attention fast. And if you are trying to influence people from afar with direct mail, e-commerce, or advertisements, capturing their attention takes on a whole new level of importance.

Thanks to technology you can generally expect people to be distracted.

In today's wired world, it is very rare to have a captive audience. When I started teaching, there were no Androids or iPhones. While passing notes in class has always been around, it is nothing compared to text messages, instant messenger, and social media. With cell phones, tablets, and computers, when I am talking to a class, I know they have access to a world of distractions right at their fingertips.

Ninety percent of American adults have cell phones, eighty percent of them text, and over sixty percent access the web from their phones (Pew, 2014). With our modern propensity to multitask, you can never assume that you have someone's complete attention. Even without technological distractions, it is possible to lose an audience to any number of distractions, even their own imagination.

The best way to handle this is to engage people however they feel comfortable. If they are starting to daydream, ask them to imagine a scenario that leads into your presentation. If they are checking their smartphone, direct them to your website or video. Instead of trying to control the interaction, roll with it and turn their energy toward your message

If you know what your audience is thinking, what they want, and what they need, it will be easier to get their attention. By tailoring your message and speaking directly to them and what makes them unique, you will have a better chance of holding their attention.

We are drowning in a world of communication, most of it impersonal. We constantly receive emails, texts, and instant messages. We are also constantly bombarded with advertising messages. And we have many interactions with people each day, most of them routine. The trick is to break through the clutter. If you are saying what everyone else is, you will not do any better than they do.

In a world full of impersonal communication, personalization is key. Dale Carnegie (1936) famously said that "a person's name is to that person the sweetest and most important sound in any language." When I talk to one of my students, I make it a point to use his or her name. It seems minor, but it really helps me connect. It lifts the conversation from routine to personal.

This holds true even when you aren't face to face. Research shows that people are more than twice as likely to open emails that include the recipient's name (Subject Line, 2013). People are more likely to open hand-addressed letters than typed ones (Pitney Bowes, 1998). With the amount of marketing material with which we are flooded, electronic and otherwise, simple personal gestures that we used to take for granted make a real difference. By using the cold reading skills we discussed earlier, you can personalize your message even more.

Since there are a variety of tools to get people's attention, there is no reason to stick with just one. Come up with a variety of techniques that lead into your message and pull out whichever one best fits your present audience.

Stories: Stories are an amazing way to build rapport. Use a story that draws your audience in and makes them want to stick around until the end. Also, if it's your story, this is a wonderful way of building authority on the topic.

Shocking facts or figures: Random trivia is interesting and can get people thinking. If there is an outrageous, obscure, or just plain weird piece of information that relates to your message, it would be a waste not to use it as a hook to draw people in.

Example: *The Truth* anti-smoking campaign gets people's attention with facts and figures such as, "Tobacco kills about 30 times more people than murder (The Truth, 2014).

Humor: People love to laugh. If you can get them with a joke or some sort of humor, you will have them on your side. Humor is a great way to make yourself likeable and get people to pay attention. Keep in mind that humor is often culture-specific. Make sure your joke is either universal or geared toward your current audience.

Rhetorical questions or hypothetical situations: Asking people to imagine what they would do or how they would feel in a particular situation is a good way of drawing them in, especially when your message is more abstract or foreign to them.

> **Example:** Financial planners often start by asking people if they are saving enough money to retire or ask them what they picture themselves doing in retirement.

Visuals: There are several learning styles and some people need more than talking. All the senses can be used to get people to stop and pay attention. Some of the best attention grabbers do not require you to say a word.

Example: Mothers Against Drunk Driving displays vehicles that were totaled in drunk driving accidents to get people's attention (MADD, 2014).

Step 2: Establish the Need

The second step is to establish the need by identifying the problem. This is an integral part of the process of influence that people often skip. Albert Einstein put it best when he said, "The formulation of the problem is often more essential than its solution." In the information age, it's not usually hard to find solutions once you understand the problem. We have a world of knowledge at our fingertips. In a few seconds I can answer almost any question. Of course, in order to do that I need to know what the actual question is.

What is the solution to my problem?

Google Search   I'm Feeling Lucky

With the massive amount of information available to the public we can all solve problems. The skill comes in defining the problems in the first place. With this paradigm shift, problem identifiers are in higher demand than problem solvers. According to a survey of employers conducted by the Conference Board (2008), the most important creative skill the employers looked for in new employees is the ability to identify and articulate problems. To address this need, schools like the University of California, Berkeley's Haas School of Business are offering courses on "Problem Finding, Problem Solving." As lecturer Sara Beckman explained, "Part of being an innovative leader is being able to frame a problem in interesting ways and to see what that problem really is before you jump into solving it" (Byrne, 2012).

Thanks to WebMD and other websites, I can find the cure to whatever ails me. The problem is that, without medical training, I seldom know what my ailment is. When I type in my symptoms I find out that it could be heartburn or cancer. The most important role of medical professionals is to identify the problem and make a diagnosis. Doctors figure out why I am nauseous. Dentists figure out why my tooth hurts. Therapists figure out why I am afraid of clowns. None of that can be found online.

Anyone can look at the grade book for my classes and identify which students are struggling. The role of a teacher, a good one anyway, is to figure out what the root problem is, why that student is having problems. Once I have figured out whether it is a problem comprehending the material, a lack of motivation, or personal problems, I can focus my efforts to help him or her succeed.

This focus on problem identification is especially important for traditional sales. There are very few products or services that people can't order online or get from another provider. Unless you are selling something totally unique and proprietary, the power generally lies with the consumers. They are relying on you and your expertise to help them figure out what they need.

I don't take my car to the mechanic to have my timing belt replaced. I take it in to find out what that strange sound is under the hood. I don't take my computer in to have the RAM increased. I take it in to figure out why it is running so slowly. And I don't go to my accountant to take advantage of specific tax deductions. I go in to find out what deductions are available. Naturally, I will continue to give them my business because these professionals have established authority, I now like them, they have helped me and I want to reciprocate, and because I want to be consistent.

A good salesperson, however, will identify a problem that the customers never knew they had. My sister always seemed to get mineral deposits on her shower door. She never really thought about it and did not realize she had a problem. One day a salesman came to her door out of the blue. He asked her if she had a problem with spots in her shower and she told him that she did. He then proceeded to explain the problem with hard water. Even though she had never given it much thought, he successfully identified the problem. It was only natural then that she would buy the water filtration system he was selling.

There are countless examples of good salespeople discovering problems, but the most extreme ones I can find are on infomercials. They often start with a black and white reenactment with terrible actors. As they overreact to the common annoyances of everyday life, the narrator says, "Don't you hate it when this happens?" or, "Have you ever had this problem?"

For example, I never knew that I had a problem of my hands getting cold when I had to take them out from under the blanket to hold my book or type on my computer. But now that they mention it, that does bother me and I definitely need a Snuggie.

The only way to address people's needs is to know what they are. Part of this has to do with just being human and relating your experiences to theirs. What problems do you generally have that other people probably share. Using the cold reading skills we discussed earlier will also be useful. The more you know about your customers, the easier it will be to identify their needs.

Among mentalists and psychics there is a list of the common human needs. The acronym for these is MATCHES, or THE SCAM if you are particularly cynical. All people focus on and are concerned with, Money, Ambition, Travel, Career, Health, Education, and Sex (Jones, 1989). If you focus on any one of these issues, you can be sure that people will be interested and will often have problems related to them. You can narrow this down even further. People have three main issues: health/wellbeing, work/money, and relationships/sex.

In 1954 Abraham Maslow, a social scientist, identified five basic human needs. After surveying people from many different cultures, subsequent researchers have updated this to include six universal needs (Tay & Diener, 2011). In no particular order they are:

Basic needs for food and shelter
Safety and security
Social support and love
Feeling respected and pride in activities
Mastery
Self-direction and autonomy

It can also be helpful to consider what your customer may be going through based on their age and gender. Look back at the section on life phases for more information about the problems they are likely facing.

Step 3: Satisfaction

Once you have established a need, the obvious next step is to satisfy the need. You are going to explain why your product or service is the best solution. We live in an age of abundance; there are countless products and services available to consumers. Your job is to make your product or service stand out. As advertising pioneer Rosser Reeves put it, you need to establish your "unique selling proposition" (Levitt, 1986). If you are selling a product, what makes it different from others on the market? If you are selling a service, what makes it better than your competitor down the street? If you are selling yourself to an employer, why are you the best candidate for the job or promotion?

The key is to establish that your product or service is somehow different. Are you less expensive than your competitors? Are you higher class? Are you cooler? Are you easier to use? Are you more reliable? What is your hook and claim to fame? Being the only person doing something or having the only product out there certainly makes this easier, but it's not necessary. Your attributes are what make your pitch and your relationships with customers unique.

There are dozens of mechanics in my area, but I always go to the same one. Any of them could change my oil, but I go to my mechanic because he comes across to me as completely honest. There are many financial advisors I could use, but I go to mine because he has the best customer service I've experienced. There are many dentists I could choose from, but I go to mine because I believe he is the most empathetic. Many people can do these jobs and can do them well. The unique, intangible assets are what set these people apart, differentiate them from others, and lead me to them my business.

I am not the only communications professor out there. There are several other people at my university that teach the same classes. We all use the same course guidelines and choose from the same stable of textbooks. What makes me unique is that I am the only communication professor that has a joke to illustrate every concept we discuss and shows students how they can read minds by using micro-expressions.

There are many speakers that help companies teach their sales forces how to increase sales. And there are many mentalists. But I am the only one that does both. If a company is just looking for a sales coach, they might not hire me. If they just want a mentalist, they might go with someone else. But if they are looking for a unique presentation that will entertain, inspire, and educate their sales force, they will naturally go with me.

Branding is everything. The most successful people in the persuasion industry are those who successfully create a distinct feeling or experience within the minds of the audience. Major companies spend millions of dollars to achieve this. Google wants to make sure that when you think about search, their brand is the first that comes to mind. The fact that people often refer to "Googling" something instead of "searching" for it means they have probably succeeded. Nike wants to make sure that when you think athletics you think of them. Mercedes wants to make sure that when you think luxury cars, they are the first name that comes to mind. All search engines search. All clothes cover our bodies (OK, maybe that isn't completely true). And most new cars run well. If we are just in the market for a car, there is no reason to buy a Mercedes. But if we want luxury and identify their brand as the most luxurious, we will naturally turn to them.

These companies have branding and marketing agencies devoted to this task. For the rest of us, however, the onus is on us. Our own personal branding sets us apart in the minds of potential customers and clients. Personal branding does not make us unique, it makes sure others know how unique we are. Ask yourself what sets you apart from the competition and make sure other people know about it. Tom Peters (1997) discussed this in his *Fast Company* article "The Brand Called You:"

> Cast aside all the usual descriptors that employees and workers depend on to locate themselves in the company structure. Forget your job title. Ask yourself: What do I do that adds remarkable, measurable, distinguished, distinctive value? Forget your job description. Ask yourself: What do I do that I am most proud of?

Coming up with your personal brand can require a bit of soul-searching and perhaps the help of others. I have come up with a series of questions that will help you define your personal brand. Take your time and don't feel like you have to answer them all right now. Get input from other people. And always feel free to change your answers as you go. This is a creative exercise and there are no wrong answers.

1. What are my core values and beliefs?

2. What energizes me or what am I passionate about?

3. What am I better at than anyone else?

4. What is my weakness or what things do I not like doing?

5. What unique life experiences have I had that set me apart? This can include upbringing, education, work, experience, etc.

6. How do I come across to others? What adjectives would they use to describe me?

7. How would someone else introduce me or how would I introduce myself?

8. How do people feel when they interact with me?

9. Why would people want to spend time with me or what problems do I solve for them?

10. What do I want to be known for?

4. Visualization

Once you have made sure that people understand the problem and know how you can help them solve it, you need to spur them to action. When the action is large or difficult, it can take a little work to get people to take that step. This is where visualization can help.

People are often stuck in the status quo. They do not know what it is like to live with the solution you are offering. If it takes an investment of time or money, it may not seem worthwhile. And if it is something they have never had or done, it might seem unattainable. Our job is to make sure people realize that the solution we offer is within reach and is well worth the investment.

My parents both went to college and got graduate degrees. As a child, college was always in my future. There was never a question as to whether I was going to go to college and graduate. For some of the first generation college students in my classes, however, success in college is not a part of their self-image. They definitely want to succeed in college, but it is not a given. They are already persuaded that college will satisfy many of their future needs and make their lives better. The next step is to help them visualize that success and believe it's possible.

The admissions department at my school had a great way of helping prospective students visualize their success. They had graduation caps and gowns mounted on the walls next to pictures of smiling graduates. They shared the importance of education and the value of our school with the prospective students, but they also helped them visualize themselves wearing those caps and gowns and walking down the aisle as successful college graduates.

People who have smoked or been out of shape for many years may have a hard time imagining themselves as non-smokers or being in shape. They may be convinced they should stop smoking or eat healthier, but actually taking action may

152

seem too difficult. If people think of themselves as smokers, giving up smoking may seem impossible, especially if they have tried and failed in the past.

If people do not see themselves as healthy, they might find it hard to take consistent action to improve their diets. Once again, if they have tried and failed, this process is even harder. The role of healthcare providers is to identify the problem and point out the solution. In some cases, however, it is also to motivate the patient to actually take action and to help them visualize success in achieving their health goals.

I don't go to my personal trainer just for guidance on how to exercise. I could find most of that information online. What makes my personal trainer good is his ability to motivate me and help me visualize a healthy and more fit me. If I can see myself succeeding, it is much more likely that I will keep plugging away. If my fitness dreams seem like a fantasy, it will be far easier to justify sleeping in rather than going to the gym.

The same thing applies to selling products. In an experiment, a researcher tried out two versions of an advertisement for a pair of running shoes. In one version the text started out with "Introducing Westerly running shoes." In the other it said, "Imagine yourself running through this park . . . [with] Westerly running shoes on your feet." Needless to say, people were more interested in buying the shoes when asked to visualize themselves wearing them (Escalas, 2007). The visualization made it real in their minds.

The status quo is powerful and people often know only what they have. I have owned cars before. If someone tried to sell me a car, I could easily imagine myself driving it. I have far more experience sitting in traffic than I want. But I have never had a boat. If someone tried to sell me a boat, I would have to imagine it. A good salesperson would help me with that.

I have never been to the Caribbean. Telling me that it is an amazing place and that I should visit might persuade me. But to really motivate me to take action, ask me to picture myself there. This allows me to incorporate "Caribbean traveler" into my self-image.

A good sales person will persuade their customer. A great one will help them visualize the results and take action. Make the product or service you are selling part of their self-image. They should be taking action not only because they are persuaded to, but because they can't imagine their life without whatever you are pitching.

5. Action

This entire chapter, and in some ways this entire book has been leading up to this section: the call to action. All your effort will be wasted if you can't get people to follow through on their commitments and make the changes they now want. It is up to you to motivate action.

You need to move from abstract agreement to taking concrete steps. Sometimes this is the one-time action of signing on the dotted line or turning over their credit card information. Often, though, change requires consistent action over time. Deciding to stay in school or get in shape requires daily action. This is why I hate the term "closing the sale." This implies that the interaction is over and there is no need for further contact. I prefer to look at the call to action as a commitment to work together or the beginning of a relationship.

There are a variety of techniques to bring about action. They will not all work with every person, so it's good to have a variety of tools to choose from. Ask yourself: what would be more effective with this person and which will leave him or her the most satisfied? With enough bravado and without any scruples, it is very easy to push people into a purchase they will regret. But if you can ethically urge people to take action that is good for both you and them, they will be less likely to have regrets and you are more likely to get referrals.

Here are some of the more common techniques:

Direct call to action is exactly what the name implies. Simply ask the person to take action. There is no need to play games. Once you have made your case for how your solution will solve someone's problem, ask him or her to act on it.

Indirect call to action is when you subtly move someone to take action by asking how the solution you offered sounds.

This is a gentler way of bringing about action and often better than being too direct, which can be perceived as pushy.

The assumptive call to action is when you assume that your customer will take action because you made such a good argument. If you are able to proceed with the right kind of confidence, this can be very effective.

The negative assumption call to action is when you ask someone if there is any reason not to take action. Naturally, if there are any reasons, you need to address them. After addressing each problem continue to ask if there are any reasons not to take action. Just be careful not to push so hard that the customer is uncomfortable.

Puppy dog call to action is when you give the product or service as a free trial. This is a great technique, especially for those with a perceiving personality, since there is no commitment. Unless your product or service is especially bad, people are unlikely to return it or discontinue it after the free trial, partially because of reciprocity.

The scarcity call to action is when you get someone to act because of impending loss. The product or service you are offering will be unavailable if he or she doesn't act soon. As we discussed in the section on scarcity, this can be because of a lack of inventory, the end of a sale, or some sort of external force.

Cradle to grave call to action is when you push for action by reminding people of the fleeting nature of time. This can be useful when people are hesitant to take action and are inclined to wait for a better day. Point out that there will never be a better time to take action and that not taking action only wastes precious time.

156

The balance sheet call to action is when you help someone come up with a list of pros and cons relative to taking action. Obviously the goal is to make the pros outweigh the cons. Make sure to do this honestly and look at both sides. Studies show that people are more likely to buy after you have pointed out a small flaw. It makes you seem more honest.

The alternate choice call to action is when you offer someone multiple choices, all of which will end in taking action. Just be careful not to make this too clever or you are likely to turn people off. Asking if someone wants to pay with cash or credit before he or she has committed to buying can ruin a sale.

The minor point call to action is when you get someone to agree to a specific point or detail and then use that to move him or her to take action. For example, a car salesperson might ask a customer if he or she would prefer the car with leather or vinyl seats. By getting people to agree to specific points, you are helping them visualize your product or service. Once again, if this is too obvious, it is likely to turn people off.

Getting people to take action is often contingent on how we frame things. There is no such thing as unframed information. Everything is relative. We make sense of the world around us through comparisons. If I told you that someone was 5'9", would you say that person is tall or short? Naturally, that would depend on framing. If this person is a child, that would be tall, for an adult it might not be. For a woman this might be tall; for a man it might be short. If this person were in Europe, it might be considered short, but in Asia it could be considered tall. More directly, whom is this person standing next to? The best way to make yourself taller is to stand next to people who are shorter than you. That is why I prefer to hang out with ugly people.

Telling your customers that you can offer them a 3.2% interest rate on their mortgage doesn't mean much until you frame it by telling them that the average is 3.8%. Or to really frame it well, you might point out that with this lower interest rate they will save enough over their 30-year mortgage to pay for their child's first year in college. Framing creates meaning out of abstract figures and can bring about action.

Sally Struthers famously called on people to donate to the Christian Children's Fund by saying that "for the price of a cup of coffee a day" you could feed a child in need. This was a brilliant way of framing the call to action. The average American spends $358 a year on coffee (Casserly, 2011). For $358 you could buy a decent television. Had she said that "for the price of a new television you can feed a child," it would not have been nearly as effective. Even though it was the same amount of money, it would have seemed very expensive. A cup of coffee a day, however, seems inconsequential.

We could tell smokers that 480,000 Americans die every year as a result of smoking, but that number doesn't mean much. We could also frame that by saying that ten times as many Americans have died from smoking than from all wars combined. We could point out that smokers die an average of ten years earlier. Or we could frame this by reminding smokers that they might not be able to see their grandchildren grow up. (CDC, 2014)

People are more motivated by losses than gains (Tversky & Kahneman, 1981). It's always nice to have more, but we generally know that we can survive with what we have. It can be scary to face the risk of losing what we have and deal with an uncertain future. For this reason, framing an action as avoiding loss is often better than framing it as a potential gain. In one study, people were asked to register for an event. One group was given a discount for registering early. The other was given a late fee if they didn't register in time. Even though the money ended up being exactly the same, more people were motivated when threatened with a loss through the late fee, than when motivated with the gain through the discount (Gächter, Orzen, Renner, & Stamer, 2009).

In many cases, emphasizing the possibility of a loss is a better way of getting someone to take action. Unless the potential gain is far greater than the loss, in the lottery for example, people are often inclined to stick with the status quo. When it comes to the potential of winning millions of dollars in a lottery, the minor loss of a few dollars seems inconsequential. Even though players have a miniscule chance of winning, by focusing on the potential and encouraging them to visualize their potential jackpot, the lottery organizers get millions of people to bet on a loser.

When it comes to more equal bets, however, the risks are often more powerful than the gains. When influencing people to save for retirement, a fear of living in poverty is more powerful than visions of wealth. When persuading people to get in shape, fear of disease is often better than visions of muscles. And sometimes emphasizing how people will miss out on a product or service is more useful than focusing on the benefits.

No matter how you go about framing your argument or calling someone to take action, make it simple. Research shows that when you give people too many options, making a choice is much harder. In one study, people in one group were offered samples from six types of jam while people in another group were offered twenty-four types of jam. Only three percent of people with more choices bought, while thirty percent of people with fewer choices bought (Iyengar & Lepper, 2000). Or to frame that differently, ten times as many people bought when they had fewer choices.

Trader Joe's, a small American grocery store chain, has taken this psychology of choice to heart. While an average grocery store typically stocks about 50,000 items, Trader Joe's only carries about 4,000 and most of them are their own brand. There is no reason to force customers to choose from a wide selection of similar products and competing brands when one will do. Thanks in part to their limited selection, Trader Joe's sells more than twice as much per square foot as Whole Foods. (Olster, 2010)

The more choices there are, the more difficult it is to decide. Our goal should be to streamline the decision making process. Don't make people redirect valuable mental energy or motivation toward deciding which of the many options to choose. Allow them to focus on one thing; taking action right now.

Conclusion

Throughout this book we have explored the intricacies of the mind. By understanding why people believe and do the things they do, our interactions just might be a little easier. My goal was to share some shortcuts that can help you understand people better and influence them more efficiently.

Now that we have this knowledge, the question is how we use it. As Voltaire said, "With great power comes great responsibility." When we know how to read people and influence their behaviors, we need to question how we will use this knowledge. Without influencing others as part of our daily interactions, nothing would ever get done. You would never get hired, your kids would never clean their rooms, patients would not take their medicine, students would not study, and the public would not buy things they need.

Sales professionals have consistently been viewed as some of the least ethical people around. People believe they use unethical tactics to trick them into buying things they do not need. Since we are all selling something, it is a constant danger that we will be labeled the same. The tools we discussed in this book are just that, tools. They can be used to help people or to take advantage of them.

When I am interacting with people and trying to persuade them I ask myself two simple questions. If they listen to me and agree to do what I'm suggesting, will they be better off?

And, when our interaction is over, will their family and community be better off than when we began? If the answer to either of these questions is no, then I know something is wrong.

Another way of looking at this is with the Four-Way test. Herbert J. Taylor created it in the early 1930s and Rotary International later adopted it (Rotary). By asking ourselves these simple questions we can make sure our actions are worthwhile.

The Four-Way Test
Of the things we think, say or do

Is it the TRUTH?

Is it FAIR to all concerned?

Will it build GOOD WILL and
BETTER FRIENDSHIPS?

Will it be BENEFICIAL
to all concerned?

During the countless interactions we have with others on a daily basis, it is relatively easy to read people and influence them. What really takes effort is making sure that we influence them for the better.

Review

Thank you for taking the time to read this book. If you enjoyed it, please take a moment to share your thoughts with others.

If you would like to receive periodic updates on my research and public appearances or find out more about the power of the mind, please go to:

www.CarlChristman.com

Extras

Extra: Lie Detection

When exploring how to read people and understand the meaning behind their body language and facial expressions, the question of lie detection always seems to come up. People are interested in figuring out whether those around them are telling the truth. Perhaps it's the influence of shows like *Lie to Me* or other crime dramas or perhaps it is a reflection of our culture.

I did not include a discussion of lie detection in the section on micro-expressions, because it can be distracting and focuses people's observations in the wrong direction. When the goal is figuring out if people are lying, our focus becomes more adversarial. We are less concerned with understanding what people think and more concerned with their possible deception.

The other problem is that detecting when people are lying is often seen as simply binary. They are either lying or telling the truth. In crime dramas, the goal is to catch someone in a lie and figure out who is guilty. In real life, it is much more complicated. In the real world there are many shades of gray.

Perhaps someone is not trying to lie to you, but they don't want to hurt your feelings. If a bored customer tries to feign interest, is that a lie? If an associate says, "We should get lunch," but doesn't really mean it, is that a lie? And if a friend asks for your input, is putting a positive spin on things really a lie?

My point is that we should be less concerned with lies and more concerned with people's feelings. If we can understand what people are thinking and feeling, then superficial issues of truth versus lies become irrelevant. By understanding micro-expressions and empathetic accuracy, you really can get inside other people's minds.

However, since lie detection is one of the most common questions I am asked, I have included a list of ten common tells that are good clues that a person is being less than truthful. One alone does not signify a lie, but, taken together, they can give you a good impression of truthfulness. Just be careful not to over-apply these tells. Upon learning them, there is a tendency to see them in every interaction. Start with the assumption that everyone is telling the truth and be very judicious in asserting that there is some form of deception going on.

Shaking Head

Shaking one's head to signify yes and no is often involuntary. As strange as it might seem, sometimes people will actually shake their heads "yes" while saying "no." This will generally not include large amounts of head movement, but a subtle, almost imperceptible, shaking.

Shrugging Shoulders

Shrugging one's shoulders often shows that someone is not sure or does not believe what he or she is saying. If someone shrugs his or her shoulders after saying something, it could signify a lack of commitment to what is being said and might be a sign of a lie.

Crossing Arms

Crossing arms can be a sign that a person is trying to create a barrier of protection. If this is done after making a statement, it could be a sign of a lie, because the person might be feeling defensive. Be careful about using just one of these as a sign of lying, because people crossing their arms could also just mean they are cold.

Turning Away

A person may turn away from you when lying or shortly thereafter. It may be as if he or she cannot face you while lying to you and is searching for an escape route after lying.

Rubbing the Face

As people lie, or shortly thereafter, they might rub their faces or play with their hair. This is a common nervous tick that people exhibit when they are uncomfortable. Since lying makes most people uncomfortable, this could be a sign of lying.

Touching Arms or Legs

People will sometimes fidget and touch their arms or legs or adjust their clothes. This can be a sign of discomfort and often indicates lying.

Hesitations

People may hesitate before speaking or repeat a question in order to buy time. If they always hesitate before speaking, this is not a sign of lying, but, if this is not typical behavior, it could mean they are trying to come up with a lie.

Changing Voice Patterns

Under stress people's voices often change, becoming higher pitched or faster, or having less clear enunciation. Since lying causes stress this might be a sign that they are being less than truthful.

Eye Contact

People usually find it hard to lie to a person while looking them in the eye. This is not always accurate, since some people don't usually make eye contact and some cultures even discourage it. But if you notice that someone who generally makes eye contact is avoiding it after a statement, this could be a sign of lying.

Looking Away

Looking away from the speaker or staring into the distance might be a sign of lying. Excessive blinking could also signify a feeling of guilt.

Extra: Culture

When exploring how to understand an audience, I made the assumption that the people you would be dealing with were from the same culture. There is no sense in complicating things by introducing variables that would not be relevant. For situations where your customers are from a different culture, however, there are a whole host of cultural differences that should be taken into account. By understanding these differences, you will have an advantage in relating to them and trying to influence them.

On a much larger scale than personality, we can see that entire cultures have specific traits. Cultures are basically groups of people that have developed their own regional or social set of customs and values that everyone abides by. What makes a culture is that most people share similar values. They are also on a fairly similar plane when it comes to the rules they live by and the social traits they share.

When communicating with people from different cultures, they may not share your personal values, traits, or social rules. The best way to effectively deal with people from another culture is to understand the broad differences between their culture and yours. Although there are many subtle differences, there are some overarching measurements that can help us frame the broader understanding of culture.

In the 1960s IBM was expanding throughout the world. When they established branch offices in various countries, they sent American employees to manage the operations. While the company made sure the employees spoke the local language fluently, they did not take into account cultural differences. As a result, in many countries, the American managers did not get along with the employees, did not get along with the suppliers, and perhaps most importantly, did not get along with the customers.

To solve this, IBM worked with Dutch social psychologist Geert Hofstede (2001) to quantify the cultural differences their organization was dealing with. After analyzing data on personal values from employees in over 70 countries, he came up with the following set of cultural variables.

Power Distance
Individualism – Collectivism
Uncertainty Avoidance
Masculinity – Femininity
Long-Term – Short-Term
Indulgence – Restraint

My research has involved applying these cultural values to the sales process. By understanding these differences, it's possible to better tailor one's sales pitch for customers in various cultures. By knowing your customer's culture, you can better address their needs and concerns. This makes is much easier to make the sale and, more importantly, make sure everyone is satisfied.

Everyone within a culture is unique, so you cannot assume that these cultural values apply equally to every individual. But this is a good starting point. More often than not, you will find that these values correctly reflect the attitudes of people within a given cultures.

Below is a detailed description of each of the six overarching cultural variables, an explanation of how they can be applied to the sales process, and a list of cultures in order based on the strength of that particular value. Please note that cultures are not simply in one category or the other when it comes to these cultural variables. It is a spectrum and they may lie anywhere along the continuum.

What is probably most useful, however, is to see where a specific culture fits in relation to your own. You are obviously not going to memorize all of this information, but it is a handy reference. If you are going to be meeting with a prospective customer or client from another culture, take a few minutes and see how their cultural values are similar to or different from your own.

Power Distance

Power distance is the amount of equality or inequality between people in a culture. A culture with a high power distance has more inequality and a more rigid hierarchy in which status or rank is very important and it's harder to advance if you are in a lower position of power. A culture with a low power distance has more equality. These cultures treat people more equally and focus less on status and rank.

High power distance cultures, like those in many Asian, Middle Eastern, and Eastern European countries, generally have more hierarchy. People in these cultures tend to have great respect for authority and typically revere those of higher rank at work, those with more education, and the elderly. They value order and those with power. Because of this, sales pitches are more effective when they play on this authority. Emphasize any certifications or licenses that you, your company, or your product or service has. Endorsements from public figures and professionals (doctors, scientists, etc.) are very useful. If you are going to use customer testimonials, make sure they are from older people, those from a higher class, or professionals. If you are speaking to a group, keep in mind that the older male is likely the decision-maker for the group.

Low power distance cultures, like America and much of Western Europe, generally have less hierarchy. People in these cultures tend to value equality. They typically revere a strong work ethic and believe that anyone can be successful with hard work. They are more likely to view those who are older, have more power, or are more educated as being different, not better. Because of this, you should make sure that your sales pitch is directed toward everyone equally. Make sure it is not perceived as condescending. Everyone wants to feel valued in the interaction. If you use endorsements or testimonials, it is better to have them from the "common person." It is better that they look like your customer or client rather than someone more powerful.

High Power Distance		**Low Power Distance**
Malaysia	France	South Africa
Slovakia	Poland	(white)
Guatemala	Hong Kong	Argentina
Panama	Belgium French	Trinidad & Tobago
Philippines	Colombia	Hungary
Russia	El Salvador	Jamaica
Romania	Turkey	Latvia
Serbia	Belgium	Lithuania
Suriname	Peru	*U.S.A.*
Venezuela	Thailand	Luxembourg
Mexico	Africa (East)	Estonia
Arab countries	Chile	Canada
China	Portugal	Netherlands
Bangladesh	Belgium/	Australia
Ecuador	Netherlands	Costa Rica
Indonesia	Uruguay	Great Britain
Africa (West)	Greece	Germany
India	South Korea	Switzerland
Singapore	Taiwan	Finland
Croatia	Iran	Sweden
Slovenia	Spain	Norway
Switzerland	Czech Republic	Ireland
(French speaking)	Malta	Switzerland
Vietnam	Pakistan	(German speaking)
Morocco	Canada	New Zealand
Bulgaria	(French speaking)	Denmark
Brazil	Japan	Israel
	Italy	Austria

Listed in order from highest power distance to lowest power distance.

Individualism – Collectivism

Individualism – collectivism is the level of individualistic or group ideals in a culture. A more individualistic culture will value individual rights and have people who define themselves based on their own personal interests and achievements. A more collectivistic culture will have people who define themselves based on the family or group and value group interests over personal rights. For those in individualistic cultures, success is defined as achieving your personal goals. For those in collectivistic cultures, success is viewed in terms of your family or group achieving its communal goals.

Individualistic cultures, like America and much of Europe, are generally made up of more independent and autonomous people. People in these cultures tend to define themselves as an individual. "I" statements are more common than "we" statements. They usually value freedom, personal time, and independent thinking. They are often motivated by individual success and praise. Because of this, sales pitches should focus on the individual, rather than the group. Highlight the individuality of your product or service and how it can make your customer stand out. Highlight their success and challenge them to do more. Why do they deserve more out of life and how can your product or service help them get it?

Collectivistic cultures, like much of Asia and Central and South America, are generally made up of cohesive social and family groups who tend to define themselves based on their group identity. "We" statements are more common than "I" statements. They usually value family, loyalty, and community. They are often motivated by group success and stability. Because of this, sales pitches should focus on the group rather than the individual. Emphasize how your product or service can help the entire family, organization, or community. Make sure you respect people's privacy and their desire not to be singled out. Keep in mind that the group, rather than an individual, may be making the buying decisions.

Individualistic

U.S.A.	Finland	Mexico
Australia	Poland	Bulgaria
Great Britain	Lithuania	Slovenia
Hungary	Luxembourg	Africa (East)
Canada	Estonia	Portugal
Netherlands	Malta	Malaysia
New Zealand	Czech Republic	Serbia
Belgium/	Austria	Hong Kong
Netherlands	Israel	Chile
Italy	Slovakia	China
Belgium	Spain	Bangladesh
Denmark	India	Africa (West)
Canada	Suriname	Singapore
(French speaking)	Morocco	Vietnam
Belgium	Japan	Thailand
(French speaking)	Argentina	El Salvador
France	Iran	South Korea
Sweden	Russia	Taiwan
Latvia	Jamaica	Peru
Ireland	Arab countries	Trinidad & Tobago
Norway	Brazil	Costa Rica
Switzerland	Turkey	Indonesia
(German speaking)	Uruguay	Pakistan
South Africa	Greece	Colombia
(white)	Croatia	Venezuela
Switzerland	Philippines	Panama
(French speaking)	Romania	Ecuador
		Guatemala
		Collectivistic

Listed in order from most individualistic to most collectivistic.

Uncertainty Avoidance

Uncertainty avoidance is the amount of tolerance people in a culture have for uncertainty. People in a culture that has high uncertainty avoidance are more likely to try to avoid uncertainty about things in their lives and their futures. These people are less likely to take risks in all areas of life. People in a culture that has low uncertainty avoidance are less concerned with knowing exactly what will happen in their lives and their futures. These people are more likely to take risks in all areas of life.

High uncertainty avoidant cultures, like Russia, are not comfortable with ambiguity. People in these cultures tend to feel threatened by uncertainty and live by stricter rules that minimize risk. They are often suspicious of change and more fearful of people or things they are not familiar with. Because of this, sales pitches should be very clear. Avoid ambiguity and make sure you use explicit language. Avoid abstract or creative arguments and stick with a predictable explanation of the benefits of your product or service.

Low uncertainty avoidant cultures, like China and America, are comfortable with ambiguity. People in these countries tend to be more adaptable and entrepreneurial. They generally value innovation and creativity. People are more likely to thrive on adventure and change. Because of this, creative sales pitches that emphasize mystery or adventure are especially successful. What makes your product or service stand out? How will it give customers a once-in-a-lifetime experience?

High Uncertainty Avoidant

Greece	Hungary	Switzerland
Portugal	Mexico	Switzerland
Guatemala	Israel	(German speaking)
Uruguay	Croatia	Trinidad & Tobago
Belgium/	Colombia	Africa (West)
Netherlands	Brazil	Netherlands
Malta	Venezuela	Africa (East)
Russia	Italy	Australia
Belgium	Czech Republic	Slovakia
El Salvador	Switzerland	Norway
Belgium	(French speaking)	New Zealand
(French speaking)	Luxembourg	South Africa
Poland	Austria	(white)
Suriname	Pakistan	Canada
Japan	Taiwan	Indonesia
Serbia	Morocco	*U.S.A.*
Romania	Arab countries	Philippines
Slovenia	Ecuador	India
Peru	Germany	Malaysia
France	Lithuania	Great Britain
Spain	Thailand	Ireland
Argentina	Latvia	China
Chile	Canada	Vietnam
Costa Rica	(French speaking)	Sweden
Panama	Estonia	Hong Kong
Turkey	Bangladesh	Denmark
Bulgaria	Finland	Jamaica
South Korea	Iran	Singapore
		Low Uncertainty Avoidant

Listed in order from highest uncertainty avoidant to lowest uncertainty avoidant.

Masculinity – Femininity

Masculinity – femininity in a culture is the amount of segregation of the roles of men and women as opposed to being more gender neutral. In a more masculine culture, men and women have specific roles that each accepts. Men usually hold positions of power and women have fewer opportunities. In a more feminine culture men and women are more equal in their roles, giving women more opportunities for advancement.

Masculine cultures, such as Japan, tend to have stricter gender roles. People in these cultures are generally more competitive and value assertiveness and achievement. They are also more likely to measure success by wealth, status, and material goods. Because of this, sales pitches should be more explicitly targeted. A sales-pitch geared toward a man would be clearly different than one geared toward a woman. Also, invoking challenges and competition can be helpful. Allowing customers to compete with others may be useful. An example of this would be offering a scarce amount of products that very few can own or scarce services that very few can access. It is useful to emphasize the status associated with possessing your product or using your service.

Feminine cultures, such as Russia and much of Northern Europe, tend to have more fluid gender roles. People in these cultures are generally more cooperative and value modesty and quality of life. They are also more likely to decide things based on consensus. Because of this, sales pitches should focus on how the product or service offered improves the quality of life for the wider group. It is better to work with your customer in a collaborative manner. Rather than selling to them, try to enlist them in a more cooperative effort to solve the problems in their community.

Masculinity

Slovakia
Japan
Hungary
South Africa
 (white)
Austria
Venezuela
Switzerland
 (German speaking)
Italy
Switzerland
Mexico
Ireland
Jamaica
Germany
Great Britain
China
Poland
Colombia
Philippines
Ecuador
U.S.A.
Australia
Belgium
 (French speaking)
Switzerland
 (French speaking)
Trinidad & Tobago

New Zealand
Greece
Czech Republic
Hong Kong
Argentina
India
Bangladesh
Belgium
Morocco
Arab countries
Canada
Luxembourg
Pakistan
Malaysia
Brazil
Singapore
Malta
Israel
Africa (West)
Indonesia
Turkey
Taiwan
Canada
 (French speaking)
Panama
Belgium/
 Netherlands
Serbia

France
Iran
Romania
Peru
Spain
Africa (East)
El Salvador
Bulgaria
Croatia
Vietnam
South Korea
Uruguay
Guatemala
Suriname
Russia
Thailand
Portugal
Estonia
Chile
Finland
Costa Rica
Slovenia
Lithuania
Denmark
Netherlands
Latvia
Norway
Sweden
Femininity

Listed in order from most masculine to most feminine.

181

Long-Term – Short-Term Orientation

Long-term and short-term orientation is how far into the future people in a culture look. People in a long-term orientated culture are more likely to look farther into the future and plan further ahead. People in a culture with a more short-term orientation are more likely to focus on the near future and are less likely to plan ahead.

As the name implies, long-term oriented cultures, like much of Asia and Eastern Europe, tend to plan long-term. People in these cultures are more likely to save for the future and save more. They generally invest in education, acquiring skills, and preparing for the next generation. Because of this, sales pitches should be very practical and offer free information. Focus on tradition and how the product or service you are offering will be of value to their family and in the future. It is better to accept payments over-timer and not try to rush things or impose time constraints and ultimatums to buy. Let people take their time and make sure they are comfortable.

Short-term cultures, like much of the Middle East, Africa, and all of the Americas, tend to focus short-term. This means that people in these cultures are less likely to save for the future and those that do save will generally save less. They are usually more focused on the latest trends and immediate gratification. They value personal fulfillment and self-actualization. Because of this, sales pitches should reflect social trends, provide recent evidence and testimonials, and provide instant gratification. Time constraints and immediate calls to action are more likely to work well for people in these cultures.

Upon completing the sale, get the goods or service to the customer as soon as possible, if only partially. There should be something concrete, like a certificate or membership card, that signifies acquisition and fulfills the desire for immediate gratification. Fast shipping and quick customer service are very important in short-term oriented cultures.

182

Long-term

South Korea
Taiwan
Japan
China
Ukraine
Germany
Estonia
Belgium
Lithuania
Russia
Belarus
Germany (East)
Slovakia
Montenegro
Switzerland
Singapore
Moldova
Czech Republic
Bosnia
Bulgaria
Latvia
Netherlands
Kyrgyzstan
Luxembourg
France
Indonesia
Macedonia
Albania
Italy
Armenia
Hong Kong
Azerbaijan
Austria

Croatia
Hungary
Vietnam
Sweden
Serbia
Romania
Great Britain
India
Pakistan
Slovenia
Spain
Bangladesh
Malta
Turkey
Greece
Brazil
Malaysia
Georgia
Finland
Poland
Israel
Canada
Saudi Arabia
Denmark
Norway
Tanzania
South Africa
New Zealand
Africa (East)
Thailand
Chile
Zambia
Portugal

Iceland
Burkina Faso
Philippines
Uruguay
Algeria
U.S.A.
Peru
Iraq
Ireland
Mexico
Uganda
Arab countries
Australia
Argentina
Mali
El Salvador
Rwanda
Jordan
Venezuela
Zimbabwe
Morocco
Iran
Dominican
 Republic
Colombia
Nigeria
Trinidad & Tobago
Africa (West)
Egypt
Ghana
Puerto Rico
Short-term

Listed in order from long-term to short-term orientation.

Indulgence - Restraint

Indulgence – restraint is a measure of how much control society imposes over human desire and gratification of human needs. Indulgent culture allow for relatively free gratification of human needs and wants and place few restrictions on people's having fun and living their lives. Restrained culture work to suppress gratification and enjoyment with strict social rules and norms.

People from indulgent cultures, like America, tend to be happier and place more emphasis on having fun and enjoying life. They tend to spend more time focusing on leisure activities and desire immediate gratification. Because of this, sales pitches should be fun. People in these cultures do not want to be lectured. They generally prefer entertaining, interactive, and one-of-a-kind presentations. Make it quick and obvious how the audience benefits.

People from restrained cultures, like much of Eastern Europe and the Middle East, tend to be more frugal, look down on indulgence, and feel that gratification should be repressed. Because of this, sales pitches should be very organized and logical. Focus on how much they can save and what the benefit is to the community. They generally prefer things to be presented more formally and in a very predictable structure. They are less likely to appreciate creative and entertaining sales pitches.

Indulgence

Venezuela	Dominican	Algeria
Mexico	Republic	Georgia
Puerto Rico	Uruguay	Hungary
El Salvador	Uganda	Italy
Nigeria	Saudi Arabia	Czech Republic
Colombia	Greece	South Korea
Trinidad & Tobago	Taiwan	Poland
Africa (West)	Turkey	Slovakia
Sweden	France	Serbia
New Zealand	Slovenia	Zimbabwe
Ghana	Peru	India
Australia	Singapore	Morocco
Cyprus	Thailand	China
Denmark	Bosnia	Azerbaijan
Great Britain	Spain	Montenegro
Canada	Jordan	Romania
Netherlands	Mali	Russia
U.S.A.	Zambia	Bangladesh
Chile	Philippines	Moldova
Iceland	Japan	Burkina Faso
Switzerland	Germany	Hong Kong
Malta	Iran	Iraq
Andorra	Africa (East)	Estonia
Ireland	Kyrgyzstan	Bulgaria
South Africa	Tanzania	Lithuania
Austria	Indonesia	Belarus
Argentina	Rwanda	Albania
Brazil	Vietnam	Ukraine
Finland	Macedonia	Latvia
Malaysia	Germany (East)	Egypt
Belgium	Arab countries	Pakistan
Luxembourg	Croatia	**Restraint**
Norway	Portugal	

Listed in order from most indulgent to most restrained.

Extra: Mind Reading Test 1

Starting on the next page, you will see pictures of people's eyes, the most expressive part of the face. Put yourself in their shoes and ask yourself how you would feel if this were your expression. Which of the four choices best describes their emotion? Write down your answers. At the end you will be able to score yourself.

This test is not timed, but try to go as fast as you can. Carefully analyzing the pictures will generally not help. Go with your instinct. If you can't identify it right away, it's unlikely that more time will help.

You may also take these tests online by going to:

www.CarlChristman.com/Empathy

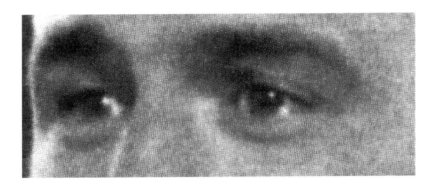

1.   decisive – anticipating – threatening – shy

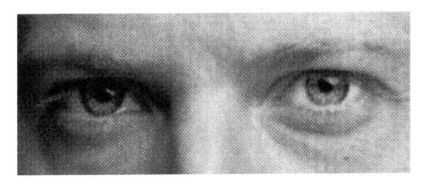

2.   irritated – disappointed – depressed – accusing

3.   contemplative – flustered – encouraging – amused

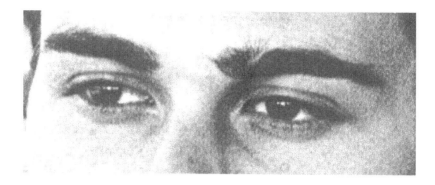

4.   **irritated – thoughtful – encouraging – sympathetic**

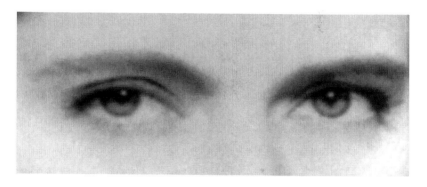

5.   **doubtful – affectionate – playful – aghast**

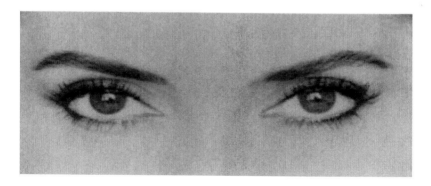

6.   **decisive – amused – aghast – bored**

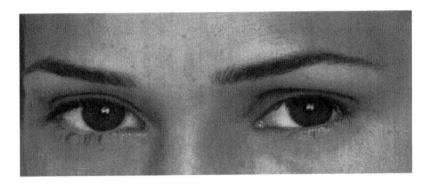

7.   arrogant – grateful – sarcastic – tentative

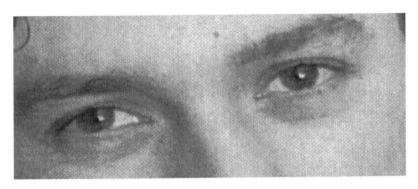

8.   dominant – friendly – guilty – horrified

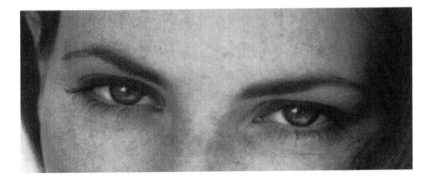

9.   embarrassed – fantasizing – confused – panicked

10.   preoccupied – grateful – insisting – imploring

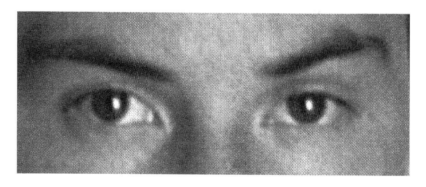

11.   contented – apologetic – defiant – curious

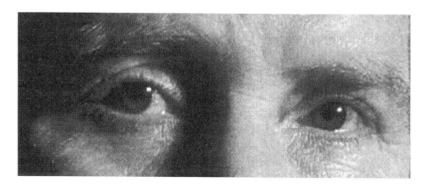

12.   pensive – irritated – excited – hostile

Compare your choices to the answers listed below and see how many you got correct.

1.	anticipating	7.	tentative
2.	accusing	8.	friendly
3.	contemplative	9.	fantasizing
4.	thoughtful	10.	preoccupied
5.	doubtful	11.	defiant
6.	decisive	12.	pensive

0 – 6   You have difficulty accurately reading people.
7 – 10   You have an average ability to read people.
11 – 12   You are very good at reading people.

This test is courtesy of Simon Baron-Cohen and his colleagues at the University of Cambridge (Baron-Cohen, Wheelwright, & Hill, 2001).

Extra: Mind Reading Test 2

Starting on the next page, you will see pictures of people's eyes, the most expressive part of the face. Put yourself in their shoes and ask yourself how you would feel if this were your expression. Which of the four choices best describes their emotion? Write down your answers. At the end you will be able to score yourself.

This test is not timed, but try to go as fast as you can. Carefully analyzing the pictures will generally not help. Go with your instinct. If you can't identify it right away, it's unlikely that more time will help.

You may also take these tests online by going to:

www.CarlChristman.com/Empathy

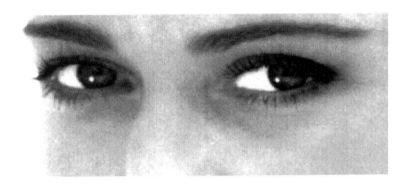

1.   panicked – incredulous – despondent – interested

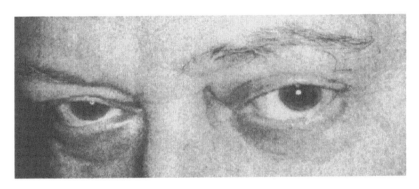

2.   alarmed – shy – hostile – anxious

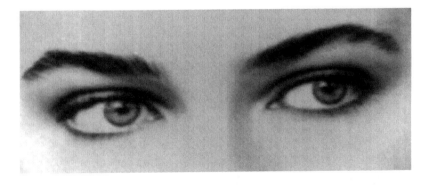

3.   joking – cautious – arrogant – reassuring

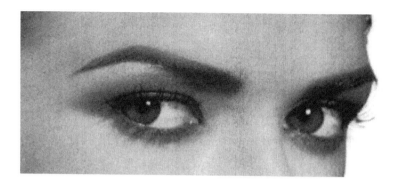

4. **interested – joking – affectionate – contented**

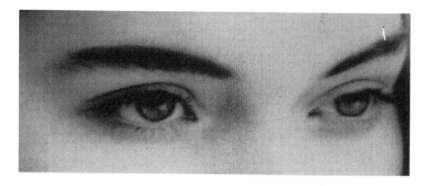

5. **impatient – aghast – irritated – reflective**

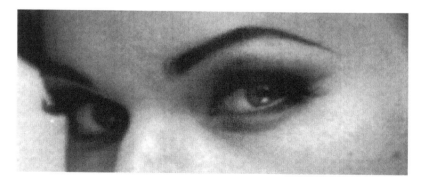

6. **grateful – flirtatious – hostile – disappointed**

7.   ashamed – confident – joking – dispirited

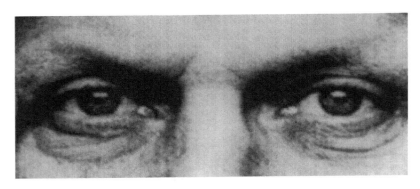

8.   serious – ashamed – bewildered – alarmed

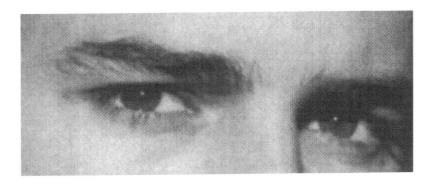

9.   embarrassed – guilty – fantasizing – concerned

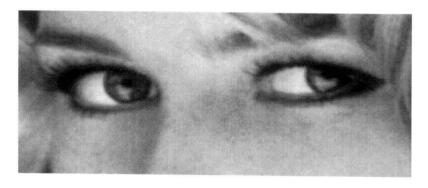

10. aghast – baffled – distrustful – terrified

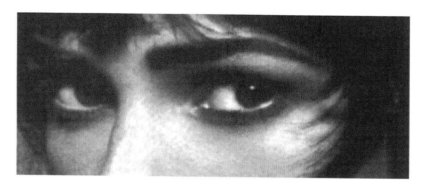

11. puzzled – nervous – insisting – contemplative

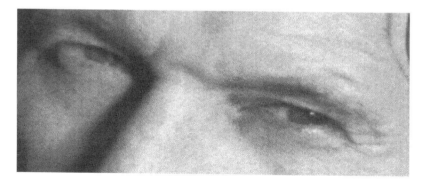

12. ashamed – nervous – suspicious – indecisive

Compare your choices to the answers listed below and see how many you got correct.

1.	interested	7.	confident
2.	hostile	8.	serious
3.	cautious	9.	concerned
4.	interested	10.	distrustful
5.	reflective	11.	nervous
6.	flirtatious	12.	suspicious

0 – 6   You have difficulty accurately reading people.
7 – 10   You have an average ability to read people.
11 – 12   You are very good at reading people.

This test is courtesy of Simon Baron-Cohen and his colleagues at the University of Cambridge (Baron-Cohen, Wheelwright, & Hill, 2001).

References

About McDonalds. (2014). Annual Reports. Retrieved from www.aboutmcdonalds.com/mcd/investors/annual_reports.ht ml

Abrams, D., Wetherell, M., Cochrane, S., Hogg, M. A., & Turner, J. C. (1990). Knowing what to think by knowing who you are. *British Journal of Social Psychology, 29*, 97-119.

Allgeier, A. R., Byrne, D., Brooks, B., & Revnes, D. (1979). The waffle phenomenon: Negative evaluations of those who shift attitudinally. *Journal of Applied Social Psychology, 9*(2), 170-182.

Allison, B., & Harkins, S. (2014, November 17). Fixed fortunes: Biggest corporate political interests spend billions, get trillions. *Sunlight Foundation.* Retrieved from www.sunlightfoundation.com/blog/2014/11/17/fixed-fortunes-biggest-corporate-political-interests-spend-billions-get-trillions/

Ansfield, M. (2007). Smiling when distressed: When a smile is a frown turned upside down. *Personality and Social Psychology Bulletin, 33*, 763–775.

Aronson, E., Wilson, T. D., & Akert, R. M. (2012). *Social Psychology (8th ed.)*. Upper Saddle River, NJ: Pearson.

Atreja, A., Fellow, N. B., & Levy, S. (2005). Strategies to enhance patient adherence: Making it simple. MedGenMed, 7(1), 4.

Baron-Cohen, S. (2009). Autism: The empathizing–systemizing (E-S) theory. *Annals of the New York Academy of Sciences,* 1156, 68–80.

Baron-Cohen, S., Wheelwright, S., & Hill, J. (2001). The "Reading the mind in the eyes" test, revised version: A study with normal adults, and adults with Asberger Syndrome or high-functioning autism. *Journal of Child Psychology and Psychiatry,* 42(2), 241-252.

Barone, D. F., Hutchings, P. S., Kimmel, H. J., Traub, H. L., Cooper, J. T., & Marshall, C. M. (2005). Increasing empathic accuracy through practice and feedback in a clinical interviewing course. *Journal of Social and Clinical Psychology,* 24(2), 156-171.

Bax, C. (2010). Entrepreneur Brownie Wise: Selling Tupperware to America's Women in the 1950s. *Journal of Women's History,* 22(2) 171-180.

Bem, D. J. (1972). Self-Perception Theory. In L. Berkowitz (Ed.), *Advances in Experimental Social Psychology: Volume 6* (pp.1-62). New York: Academic Press.

Benson, P. L., Karabenic, S. A., & Lerner, R. M. (1976). Pretty pleases: The effects of physical attractiveness on race, sex, and receiving help. *Journal of Experimental Social Psychology,* 12(5), 409-415.

Bickman, L. (1974). The social power of a uniform. *Journal of Applied Social Psychology,* 4(1), 47-61.

Blaker, B. M., Rompa, I., Dessing, I., Vriend, A. F., Herschberg, C., & Van Vugt, M., (2013). The height leadership advantage in men and women: Testing evolutionary psychology predictions about the perceptions of tall leaders. *Group Processes and Intergroup Relations,* 16(1), 17-27.

Bond, M. H., & Smith, P. B. (1996). Culture and conformity: A meta-analysis of studies using Asch's (1952b, 1956) line judgment task. *Psychological Bulletin,* 119(1), 111-137.

Bornstein, R. F., Leone, D. R., & Gallery, D. J. (1987). The generalizability of subliminal mere exposure effects. *Journal of Personality and Social Psychology,* 53(6), 1070-1079.

Brock, S. (1994). *Using Type in Selling: Building Customer Relationships with the Myers-Briggs Type Indicator.* Mountain View, CA: Consulting Psychologists Press.

Budesheim, T. L., & DePaola, S. J. (1994). Beauty or the beast? The effects of appearance, personality, and issue information on evaluations of political candidates. *Personality and Social Psychology Bulletin,* 20(4), 339-348.

Burger, J. M., Messian, N., Patel, S., del Prado, A., & Anderson, C. (2004). What a coincidence! The effects of incidental similarity on compliance. *Personality and Social Psychology Bulletin,* 30(1), 35-43.

Byrne, J. (2012, November 24). How spaghetti & marshmallows are being used to teach creative problem framing at Hass. *Poets & Quants.* Retrieved from www.poetsandquants.com/2012/11/24/how-spaghetti-marshmallows-tape-are-being-used-to-teach-creative-problem-framing-at-haas/

Caesar, C. (2014, August 21). 100s of customers pay for each others' Starbucks: 1 jerk ruins it all. *Boston Globe.*

Calculators: Life Expectancy. *Social Security.* Retrieved from www.ssa.gov/planners/lifeexpectancy.htm

Carducci, B. J., Deuser, P. S., Bauer, A., Large, M., & Ramaekers, M. (1989). An application of the foot in the door technique to organ donation. *Journal of Business and Psychology,* 4(2), 245–249.

Casserly, M. (2011, July 15). The $32,000 cup of coffee and other lifetime spending mistakes. *Forbes.*

CDC. (2014). 2014 surgeon general's report: The health consequences of smoking—50 years of progress. *Centers for Disease Control.* Retrieved from www.cdc.gov/tobacco/data_statistics/sgr/50th-anniversary/index.htm

Cesarani, D. (2005). *Eichmann: His Life and Crimes.* London: Vintage.

Chaiken, S. (1979). Communicator physical attractiveness and persuasion. *Journal of Personality and Social Psychology,* 37(8), 1387-1397.

Chan, A. (2014, August 22). Cheap bastard ends 10 hours of Starbucks customers "Paying it Forward." *Gawker.* Retrieved from www.gawker.com/cheap-bastard-ends-10-hours-of-starbucks-customers-pay-1625511330

Christakis, N., & Fowler, J. (2008). The collective dynamics of smoking in a large social network. *New England Journal of Medicine,* 358, 2249-2258.

Cialdini, R. B. (2009). *Influence: Science and Practice. (5ᵗʰ ed.).* Boston: Pearson Education, Inc.

Cialdini, R. B., & Martin, S. (2012). Secrets from the Science of Persuasion. *Influence at Work.* Retrieved from www.youtube.com/watch?v=cFdCzN7RYbw

Colvin, C. R., Vogt, D. S., & Ickes, W. (1997). Why do friends understand each other better than strangers do? In W. Ickes (Ed.), *Empathic accuracy* (pp. 169-193). New York: Guilford Press.

The Conference Board. (2008, October). Ready to innovate: Are educators and executives aligned on the creative readiness of the U.S. workforce? Retrieved from www.americansforthearts.org/sites/default/files/pdf/informa tion_services/research/policy_roundtable/ReadytoInnovateF ull.pdf

Coster, H. (2009, August 21). Companies seek a fresh start with new names. *Forbes.* 8/21/2009.

Dawkins, R. (2006). *The God Delusion.* London: Bantam Press.

Decety, J., & Skelly, L. (2013). The Neural Underpinnings of the Experience of Empathy: Lessons for Psychopathy. In K. N. Ochsner and S. M. Kosslyn (Eds.), *The Oxford Handbook of Cognitive Neuroscience: Volume 2* (pp. 228-243). New York: Oxford University Press.

Doja, A., & Roberts, W. (2006). Immunizations and autism: A review of the literature. *Canadian Journal of Neurological*

Science, 33(4), 341–346.

Dolin, D. J., & Booth-Butterfield, S. (1995). Foot-in-the-door and cancer prevention. *Health Communication, 7*(1), 55-66.

Drachman, D., deCarufel, A., & Inkso, C. A. (1978). The extra credit effect in interpersonal attraction. *Journal of Experimental Social Psychology, 14*(5), 458-467.

Dworman, S. (2003). *$12 Billion of Inside Marketing Secrets: Discovered Through Direct Response Television Sales.* Los Angeles: SDE Publishing.

Dwyer, J. (2010, January 5). A clothing clearance where more than just the prices have been slashed. *New York Times.*

Ekman, P. (2007). *Emotions Revealed (2nd ed.).* New York: Henry Hold and Company.

Ekman, P., & Friesen, W. (1978). *Facial Action Coding System: A Technique for the Measurement of Facial Movement.* Palo Alto, CA: Consulting Psychologists Press.

Ekman, P., & Friesen, W. V. (1969). The repertoire of nonverbal behavior: Categories, origins, usage, and coding. *Semiotica, 1*(1), 49-98.

Elfenbein, H. A., & Ambady, N. (2002). On the universality and cultural specificity of emotion recognition: A meta-analysis. *Psychological Bulletin, 128*(2), 203-235.

Emswiller, T., Deaux, K., & Willits, J. E. (1971). Similarity, sex, and requests for small favors. *Journal of Applied Social Psychology, 1*(3), 284-291.

Escalas, J. E. (2007). Self-referencing and persuasion:

Narrative transportation versus analytical elaboration. *Journal of Consumer Research*, 33(March), 421-429.

Evans, F.B. (1963). *American Behavioral Scientists*, 6(7), 76-79.

Fang, X., Singh, S., & Ahulwailia, R. (2007). An examination of different explanations for the mere exposure effect. *Journal of Consumer Research*, 34(June), 97-103.

Fehr, E., & Gächter, S. (2000). Fairness and retaliation: The economics of reciprocity. *Journal of Economic Perspectives*, 14(3), 159–181.

Feintzeig, R. (2014, June 9). Want to be CEO? Stand tall. *The Wall Street Journal*.

Festinger, L. (1957). *A Theory of Cognitive Dissonance*. California: Stanford University Press.

Freedman, J. L., & Fraser, S. C. (1966). Compliance without pressure: The foot-in-the-door technique. *Journal of Personality and Social Psychology*, 4(2), 195-202.

Frenzen, J. R., & Davis, H. L. (1990). Purchasing behavior in embedded markets. *Journal of Consumer Research*, 17(June), 1-12.

Gächter, S., Orzen, H., Renner, E., & Stamer, C. (2009). Are experimental economists prone to framing effects? A natural field experiment. *Journal of Economic Behavior & Organization*, 70(3), 443-446.

Galati, D., Sini, B., Schmidt, S., & Tinti, C. (2003). Spontaneous facial expressions in congenitally blind and sighted children aged 8-11. *Journal of Visual Impairment and Blindness,* 97(7), 418-428.

Gallup Poll. (2013, December). Honesty / ethics in professions. Retrieved from www.gallup.com/poll/1654/honesty-ethics-professions.aspx

Garthwaite, C., & Moore, T. (2008). The role of celebrity endorsements in politics: Oprah, Obama, and the 2008 Democratic primary. *The Journal of Law, Economics, & Organization,* 29(2).

Gleason, K. A., Jensen-Campbell, L. A., & Ickes, W. (2009). The role of empathic accuracy in adolescents' peer relations and adjustment. *Personality and Social Psychology Bulletin,* 35(8), 997-1011.

Goldstein, N. J., Cialdini, R., B., & Griskevicius, V. (2008). A room with a viewpoint: Using social norms to motivate environmental conservation in hotels, *Journal of Consumer Research,* 35(3), 472-482.

Gruner, S. (1996, November 1). Reward good customers. *Inc.*

Grush, J. E., McKeough, K. L., & Ahlering, R. F. (1978). Extrapolating laboratory exposure experiments to actual political elections. *Journal of Personality and Social Psychology,* 36(3), 257-270.

Hamby, P., & Malveaux, S. (2007, December 9). Thanks to Oprah, Obama camp claims biggest crowd yet. *CNN.* Retrieved from www.cnn.com/2007/POLITICS/12/09/oprah.obama/

Hammermesh, D., & Biddle, J. E. (1994). Beauty and the labor market. *The American Economic Review,* 84(5), 1174-1194.

Harris Polls. (2013). American's Belief in God, Miracles and Heaven Declines. Retrieved from www.harrisinteractive. com/NewsRoom/HarrisPolls/tabid/447/ctl/ReadCustom%20 Default/mid/1508/ArticleId/1353/Default.aspx

Hays, C. (2005). *The Real Thing: Truth and Power at the Coca-Cola Company.* New York: Random House.

Hecht, M., & LaFrance, M. (1998). License or obligation to smile: The effect of power and sex on amount and type of smiling. *Personality and Social Psychology Bulletin,* 24(12), 1332–1342.

Hofstede, G. (2001). *Culture's Consequences : Comparing Values, Behaviors, Institutions, and Organizations Across Nations.* Thousand Oaks, CA: Sage Publications.

Hofstede, G., Hofstede, G. J., & Minkov, M. (2010). *Cultures and Organizations: Software of the Mind.* New York: McGraw Hill.

Hornbuckle, D. (2009, August). The Oprah Effect. *Inc.*

Howard, D. J., Gengler, C., & Jain, A. (1995). What's in a Name? A complimentary means of persuasion. *Journal of Consumer Research,* 22(2), 200-211.

Hymowitz, K., Carroll, J., Wilcox, W., & Kaye, W. (2013). The Benefits and Costs of Delayed Marriage in America. *Knot Yet.* Retrieved from www.twentysomethingmarriage .org

Ickes, W. (2003). *Everyday Mind Reading: Understanding What Other People Think and Feel.* Amherst, NY: Prometheus Books.

Ickes, W., Gesn, P. R., & Graham, T. (2000). Gender differences in empathic accuracy: Differential ability or differential motivation? *Personal Relationships, 7*(1), 95-110.

Ickes, W., Stinson, L., Bissonnette, V., & Garcia, S. (1990). Naturalistic social cognition: Methodology, assessment, and validation. *Journal of Personality and Social Psychology, 51*(1), 66-82.

Ickes, W., & Tooke, W. (1988). The Observational Method: Studying the Interaction of Minds and Bodies. In S. Duck, D. Hay, S. Hobfoll, W. Ickes, & B. Montgomery (Eds.), *The Handbook of Personal Relationships: Theory, Research and Interventions* (pp. 79-97). Chichester, England: John Wiley.

Iyengar, S. S., & Lepper, M. R. (2000). When choice is demotivating: Can one desire too much of a good thing? *Journal of Personality and Social Psychology, 79*(6), 995-1006.

Jones, B. (1989). *King of the Cold Readers: Advanced Professional Pseudo-Psychic Techniques.* Bakersfield, CA: Jeff Busby Magic, Inc.

Kanfer, S. (1995). *The Last Empire: De Beers, Diamonds, and the World.* New York: Farrar, Straus and Giroux.

Keirsey, D. (1998). *Please understand me II : Temperament, Character, Intelligence.* Irvine, CA: Prometheus Nemesis Book Company.

"Kerry discusses $87 billion comment." (2004, September 30). CNN. Retrieved from www.cnn.com/2004/ALLPOLITICS /09/30/kerry.comment

King, L. A., & Emmons, R. A. (1990). Conflict over emotional expression: Psychological and physical correlates. *Journal of Personality and Social Psychology,* 58(5), 864-877.

Klein, K. J. K., & Hodges, S. D. (2001). Gender differences, motivation, and empathic accuracy: When it pays to understand. *Personality and Social Psychology Bulletin,* 27(6), 720-730.

Lefkowitz, M., Blake, R. R., & Mouton, J. S. (1955). Status factors in pedestrian violations of traffic signals. *Journal of Abnormal and Social Psychology,* 51(3), 704-706.

Levitt, T. (1986). *The Marketing Imagination (New, expanded edition).* New York: Free Press.

Lynn, M. (1989). Scarcity effect on value: Mediated by assumed expensiveness. *Journal of Economic Psychology,* 10(2), 257-274.

Mack, D., & Rainey, D. (1990). Female applicants' grooming and personal selection. *Journal of Social Behavior and Personality,* 5(5), 399-407.

Marangoni, C., Garcia, S., Ickes, W., & Teng, G. (1995). Empathic accuracy in a clinically relevant setting. *Journal of Personality and Social Psychology,* 68(5), 854-869.

Maslow, A. H. (1954). *Motivation and Personality.* New York: Harper and Row.

Masnick, M. (2005, January 5). Since when is it illegal to just mention a trademark online? *Tech Dirt.* Retrieved from www.techdirt.com/articles/20050105/0132239.shtml

Matsumoto, D., Frank, M. G., & Hwang, H. S. (2013).

Nonverbal Communication: Science and Application. Thousand Oaks, CA: Sage Publications.

Mauro, R. (1984). The constable's new clothes: Effects of uniforms on perceptions and problems of police officers. *Journal of Applied Social Psychology,* 14(1), 42-56.

McClure, S. M., Li, J., Tomlin, D., Cypert, K., Montague, L. M., & Montague, P. R. (2004). Neural correlates of behavioral preference for culturally familiar drinks. *Cell,* 44(2), 379-387.

Michaelson, E. (2012, May 4). Disneyland's Club 33 opens up waitlist. ABC7.com. Retrieved from www.abc7.com/ archive/8647966

Milgram, S. (1963). Behavioral study of obedience. *Journal of Abnormal and Social Psychology,* 67(4), 371-378.

Milgram, S. (1974). *The Obedience to Authority: An Experimental View.* New York: Harper Collins.

Miller, A. (1949). *Death of a Salesman.* New York: Viking Press.

Monahan, J. L., Murphy, S. T., & Zajonc, R. B. (2000). Subliminal mere exposure: Specific, general, and diffuse effects. *Psychological Science,* 11(6), 462-466.

Nyhan, B., Reifler, J., Richey, S., & Freed, G. (2014). Effective messages in vaccine promotion: A randomized trial. *Pediatrics,* (March 3).

Olson, I. R., & Marshuetz, C. (2005). Facial attractiveness is appraised in a glance. *Emotion,* 5(4), 498-502.

Olster. S. (2010, August 23). Inside the secret world of Trader Joe's. *Fortune.*

Osram Sylvania. (2013). Sylvania socket survey. Retrieved from www.sylvania.com/en-us/tools-and-resources/surveys/Pages/socket-survey.aspx

Pallak, M. S., Cook, D. A., & Sullivan, J. J. (1980). Commitment and Energy Conservation. In L. Bickman (Ed.), Applied Social Psychology Annual (pp. 235-253). Thousand Oaks, CA: Sage Publications.

Peers, A. (2012, January). Qatar purchases Cézanne's "The Card Players for more than $250 million, highest price ever for a work of art. *Vanity Fair.*

Peters, T. (1997 August/September). The brand called you. *Fast Company.*

Pickett, C. L., Gardner, W. L., & Knowles, M. (2004). Getting a cue: The need to belong and enhanced sensitivity to social cues. *Personality and Social Psychology Bulletin,* 30(9), 1095-1107.

Pink, D. (2012). *To Sell is Human.* New York: Riverhead Books.

Przybylski, A., Murayama, K., DeHaan, C. R., & Gladwell, V. (2013), Motivational, emotional, and behavioral correlates of fear of missing out. *Computers in Human Behavior,* 29(4), 1814–1848.

Regan, R. T. (1971). Effects of a favor and liking on compliance. *Journal of Experimental Social Psychology,* 7, 627–639.

Reinhold, R. (1997). Myers Briggs Test: What is your Myers-Briggs Personality Type? *Personality Pathways.* Retrieved from hwww.personalitypathways.com/type_inventory.html

Ridley, M. (1997). *The Origin of Virtue: Human Instincts and the Evolution of Cooperation.* London: Penguin Books.

Ritts, V., Patterson, M. L., & Tubbs, M. E. (1992). Expectations, impressions, and judgments of physically attractive students: A review. *Review of Educational Research,* 62(4), 413-426.

Roeyers, H., Buysse, A., Ponnet, K., & Pichal, B. (2001). Advancing advanced mind-reading tests: Empathic accuracy in adults with a pervasive developmental disorder. *Journal of Child Psychology and Psychiatry,* 42(2), 271-278.

Rogers, P. (2003, June 24). Photo of Streisand home becomes an Internet hit. *San Jose Mercury News.*

Ronay, R., & Carney, D. R. (2012). Testosterone's negative relationship with empathic accuracy and perceived leadership ability. *Social Psychological and Personality Science,* 4(1), 92-99.

Rotary Global History Fellowship. Retrieved from www.rotaryfirst100.org/presidents/1954taylor/bio.htm#.VK DVwAMAg

Rowland, I. (2008). *The Full Facts Book of Cold Reading: A Comprehensive Guide to the Most Persuasive Psychological Manipulation Technique in the World (4th ed.).* London: Ian Rowland Limited.

Schultz, P. W. (1999). Changing behavior with normative feedback interventions: A field experiment on curbside recycling. *Basic and Applied Social Psychology,* 21(1), 25-38.

Schwarz, N. (1984). When reactance effects persist despite restoration of freedom: Investigations of time delay and vicarious control. *European Journal of Social Psychology,* 14(4), 405-419.

Sheehy, G. (1995). *New Passages: Mapping Your Life Across Time.* New York: Random House.

Sheehy, G. (1976). *Passages: Predictable Crises of Adult Life.* New York: Bantam.

Sherman, S. J. (1980). On the self-erasing nature of errors of prediction. *Journal of Personality and Social Psychology,* 39(2), 211–221.

Shtulman, A., & Valcarcel, J. (2012). Scientific knowledge suppresses but does not supplant earlier intuitions. *Cognition,* 124(2), 209–215.

Siegel, M. (2006). *Bird Flu: Everything You Need to Know About the Next Pandemic.* Hoboken, NJ: Wiley

Silverman, R. (2014, Octoer 2). Some ice-bucket challenge funds will go to research. *The Wall Street Journal.*

Simpson, J. A., Ickes, W., & Blackstone, T. (1995). When the head protects the heart: Empathic accuracy in dating relationships. *Journal of Personality and Social Psychology,* 69(4), 629.

Social Security History. *Social Security.* Retrieved from

www.ssa.gov/history/lifeexpect.html

Stewart, J. E., II. (1980). Defendant's attractiveness as a factor in the outcome of trials. *Journal of Applied Social Psychology*, 10(4), 348-361.

Strohmetz, D. B., Rind, B., Fisher, R., & Lynn, M. (2002). Sweetening the till: The use of candy to increase restaurant tipping. *Journal of Applied Social Psychology*, 32(2), 300-309.

Stulp, G., Buunk, A. P., Verhulst, S., & Pollet, T. V. (2013). Tall claims? Sense and nonsense about the importance of height of US presidents. *Leadership Quarterly*, 24(1). 159-171.

Tay, L., & Diener, E. (2011). Needs and subjective well-being around the world. *Journal of Personality and Social Psychology*, 101(2), 354-365.

Taylor, R. (1978). Marilyn's friends and Rita's customers: A study of party selling as play and as work. *Sociological Review*, 26(3), 573-611.

Taylor, T., & Booth-Butterfield, S. (1993). Getting a foot in the door with drinking and driving: A field study of healthy influence. *Communication Research Reports*, 10(1), 95-101.

Tooby, J. & Cosmides, L. (2008). The Evolutionary Psychology of the Emotions and their Relationship to Internal Regulatory Variables. In M. Lewis, J. M. Haviland-Jones, & L. Feldman Barrett, (Eds.) Handbook of Emotions, (3rd Ed.). NY: Guilford.

Trivers, R. (1971). The evolution of reciprocal altruism. *The Quarterly Review of Biology*, 46(1), 35-57.

Tversky, A., & Kahneman, D. (1981). The framing of decisions and the psychology of choice. *Science,* 211 (4481), 453–458.

Ubel, P. (2008, December 18). eBay and the brain: What psychology teaches us about the economic downturn. *Scientific American.*

U.S. Beverage Results for 2013. (2014, March 31). *Beverage Digest,* 65(7).

U.S. Bureau of Labor Statistics. (2013, May). Economic news release. Retrieved from www.bls.gov/news.release/ ocwage.t01.htm

Verhofstadt, L. L., Buysse, A., Ickes, W., Davis, M., &Devoldre, I. (2008). Support provision in marriage: The role of emotional linkage and empathic accuracy. *Emotion,* 8(6), 792-802.

Wagner, M. (2014, August 23). 'I had to put an end to it': Florida curmudgeon intentionally breaks 458-person pay-it-forward chain at Starbucks. *New York Daily News.*

Wazana, A. (2000). Physicians and the pharmaceutical industry: Is a gift ever just a gift? *Journal of the American Medical Association,* 283(3), 373-380.

Wedekind, C., & Milinski, M. (2000). Cooperation through image scoring in humans. *Science,* 288(5467), 850-852.

Weitzman, E., Nelson, T., & Wechsler, H. (2003). Taking up binge drinking in college: The influences of person, social group, and environment. *Journal of Adolescent Health,* 32(1), 26-35.

Worchel, S. (1992). Beyond a commodity theory analysis of censorship: When abundance and personalism enhance scarcity effects. *Basic and Applied Social Psychology*, 13(1), 79-92.

Worchel, S., Lee, J., & Adewole, A. (1975). Effects of supply and demand on ratings of object value. *Journal of Personality and Social Psychology*, 32(5), 906-914.

Yglesias, M. (2013, August 9). Sweet Sorrow: Coke won the cola wars because great taste takes more than a single sip. *Slate*.

Zellinger, D. A., Fromkin, H. L., Speller, D. E., & Kohn, C. A. (1975). A commodity theory analysis of the effects of age restrictions upon pornographic materials. *Journal of Applied Psychology*, 60(1), 94-99.

Image References

Facial expression images feature Ruben Padilla (2015).

Mind reading test pictures courtesy of Simon Baron-Cohen and his colleagues at the University of Cambridge. (2001)

Dogs playing poker by Cassius Marcellus Coolidge (1903).

The Creation of Adam by Michelangelo di Lodovico Buonarroti Simoni (1511-1512).

Salvador Dali picture by Roger Higgins for World Telegram (1965).

Florence Owens Thompson picture by Dorothea Lange for the Farm Security Administration (1936).

Che Guevara picture by Alberto Korda (1960).

Jonestown image from The Jonestown Institute (1978).

ALS image by the ALS Association.

Celebrity selfie by Bradley Cooper and Ellen DeGeneres for AMPAS and ABC (2014).

Hotels.com image by Hotels.com L.P.

Barack Obama, Michelle Obama & Oprah Winfrey picture by Pete Souza for the White House (2011).

Pepsi Challenge image from PepsiCo.

Barack Obama and Mitt Romney picture by Photo Works, Maria Dryfhout, Spirit of America & Shutterstock.com for US News and World Reports (2012).

Magic Castle picture from the Academy of Magical Arts.

The Interview image from Sony Pictures.

The Card Players by Paul Cézanne (1894-1895).

Disney Vault image from The Walt Disney Company.

Barbra Streisand house picture by Kenneth & Gabrielle Adelman of the California Coastal Records Project.

Sacrifice of Isaac by Caravaggio (1603).

Stanley Milgram picture from Yale University.

Razor advertisement from Braun.

Drunk driving display vehicle from MADD.

Google search image from Google.

Snuggie image from Allstar Products Group.

Pinocchio image from Walt Disney Productions (1940).

25755090R00123

Made in the USA
San Bernardino, CA
10 November 2015